THE COMPLETE GUIDE TO
OCEAN LIFE

Sandy Creek

An Imprint of Sterling Publishing
387 Park Avenue South
New York, NY 10016

ISBN: 978-1-4351-4408-8 (print format)

A CIP record for this book is available from the Library of Congress.

For information about custom editions, special sales, and premium and corporate purchases, please contact Sterling Special Sales at 800-805-5489 or specialsales@sterlingpublishing.com.

Manufactured in China
Lot #:
10 9 8 7 6 5 4 3 2 1
09/12

Picture Credits

Key: C=Corbis/ F=FLPA/ G=Getty/ N=Nature Picture library/ S=Shutterstock/ SPL=Science Photo Library

CORBIS

1 Visuals Unlimited, 7t Richard Du Toit/Minden Pictures, 12-13 Visuals Unlimited, 30-31 Norbert Wu/Minden Pictures, 31t Jonathan Blair, 41t Tony Arruza, 42-43 Robert Harding Specialist Stock, 47t Lawson Wood, 50-51 Hoberman Collection, 54-55 Brandon D. Cole, 55c Norbert Wu/Science Faction, 86 Norbert Wu/Minden Pictures,

98-99 Ralph White, 98b Ralph White, 99t Ralph White, 111t Paul Souders, 126t Jean-Daniel Sudres/Hemis

FLPA

2-3 Jan Vermeer, 4-5 Birgitte Wilms/Minden Pictures, 4t Kevin Schafer, 5b Malcolm Schuyl, 5t Birgitte Wilms. 6-7 Reinhard Dirscherl, . 8-9 Imagebroker, 9t Michio Hoshino/Minden Pictures, 9b Mike Parry/Minden Pictures. 10-11 Reinhard Dirscherl, 10b Norbert Probst/Imagebroker, 11c Norbert Wu/Minden Pictures, 12b Gerard Lacz, 13b Fred Bavendam/Minden Pictures. 14-15 FotoNatura/FN/Minden, 14b David Hosking, 15t Malcolm Schuyl, 15b Jules Cox. 16-17 Biosphoto, Thierry Montford/Biosphoto, 17t Tui De Roy, 17b Tui De Roy/Minden Pictures. 18-19 David Pattyn/Minden Pictures, 18b Tui De Roy/Minden Pictures, 19t Neil Bowman. 20-21 Imagebroker, 21t Scott Leslie/Minden Pictures, 21b J.W.Alker/Imagebroker. 22-23 Reinhard Dirscherl, 22b Imagebroker, 23t ImageBroker. 24-25 D P Wilson, 24b Fred Bavendam/Minden Pictures, 25t Norbert Wu/Minden Pictures. 26-27 Chris Newbert/Minden Pictures, 26b ImageBroker, 27c Pete Oxford/Minden Pictures. 28-29 Reinhard Dirscherl, 29t Reinhard Dirscherl, 31b Ingo Arndt/Minden Pictures. 32 Colin Marshall, 33t Chris Newbert/Minden Pictures, , 33b ImageBroker, 34-35 Mitsuaki Iwago/Minden Pictures, 35t Norbert Probst/Imagebroker, 35b Frans Lanting. 36-37 Chris Newbert/Minden Pictures, 37t Hiroya Minakuchi/Minden Pictures, 37b Panda Photo. 38-39 Flip Nicklin/Minden Pictures, 38b D P Wilson, 39t D P Wilson. 40 Reinhard Dirscherl, 41b Ingo Arndt/Minden Pictures, 43t Hiroya Minakuchi/Minden Pictures, 43b Albert Visage. 44-45 Sergey Gorshkov/Minden Pictures, 45t Imagebroker, 45b NielsDK/Imagebroker, 46-47 Colin Marshall, 46c Colin Marshall, 48-49 Richard Herrmann/Minden Pictures, 49t Hiroya Minakuchi/Minden Pictures, 49b Suzi Eszterhas/Minden Pictures, 51t Ingo Arndt/Minden Pictures. 50-51 Norbert Wu/Minden Pictures, 53t Colin Marshall, 53b Derek Middleton, 54b Norbert Wu/Minden Pictures, 56-57 Fred Bavendam/Minden Pictures, 56c Colin Marshall, 56b Fred Bavendam/Minden Pictures, 57c Imagebroker. 58-59 Malcolm Schuyl, 59t Norbert Wu/Minden Pictures, 59b Birgitte Wilms/Minden Pictures. 60-61 ImageBroker, 61t Imagebroker,Norbert Probst, 61b Norbert Wu/Minden Pictures. 60-61 Fred Bavendam/Minden Pictures, 62c Norbert Wu/Minden Pictures, 63b Norbert Wu/Minden Pictures. 64-65 Mike Parry/Minden Pictures, 64b Mike Parry/Minden Pictures, 65b Reinhard Dirscherl. 66-67 Reinhard Dirscherl, 67t Colin Munro, 67b Panda Photo. 68-67 Norbert Probst/Imagebroker, 70-71 Patricio Robles Gil/Minden Pictures, 70c A© Biosphoto, Christopher Swann/Biosphoto/, 71c Malcolm Schuyl. 72-73 Colin Marshall, 72 Colin Marshall, 73b Panda Photo. 74 Norbert Wu/Minden Pictures, 74b Hiroya Minakuchi/Minden Pictures, 75 Panda Photo. 76-77 Richard Du Toit/Minden Pictures, 76b Malcolm Schuyl, 77t Gilles Barbier/Imagebroker. 78-79 Colin Marshall, 79t Hiroya Minakuchi/Minden Pictures, 79b Flip Nicklin/Minden Pictures. 80-81 Terry Whittaker, 80b Jurgen & Christine Sohns, 81t: Norbert Probst/Imagebroker. 82-83 Richard Herrmann/

Minden Pictures, 82b Flip Nicklin/Minden Pictures, 83t Hiroya Minakuchi/Minden Pictures. 84-85 Hiroya Minakuchi/Minden Pictures, 84b Theo Allofs/Biosphoto, 85b Flip Nicklin/Minden Pictures, 87b Norbert Wu/Minden Pictures. 88 Reinhard Dirscherl, 89b Norbert Wu/Minden Pictures. 90 Norbert Wu/Minden Pictures, 91t Photo Researchers, 91b Norbert Wu/Minden Pictures. 92b Norbert Wu/Minden Pictures, 93t Norbert Wu/Minden Pictures, 93b FNorbert Wu/Minden Pictures, 94c Norbert Wu/Minden Pictures, 95c Steve Trewhella. 96-97 Reinhard Dirscherl, 97t Jonh Weeber/Minden Pictures, 97b Reinhard Dirscherl. 100-101 Imagebroker, Gabrielle Therin-Wei, 100b Jules Cox, 101b Mitsuaki Iwago/Minden Pictures. 102-103 Dickie Duckett, 103t Flip Nicklin/Minden Pictures, 103b Pete Oxford/Minden Pictures. 104-105 Richard Herrmann/Minden Pictures, 105c Flip Nicklin/Minden Pictures, 105b Flip Nicklin/Minden Pictures. 106-107 Flip Nicklin/Minden Pictures. 106b Flip Nicklin/Minden Pictures, 107b Flip Nicklin/Minden Pictures. 108-109 Jan Vermeer/Minden Pictures, 108b Yva Momatiuk, John Eastcott/Minden Pictures, 109t Jan Vermeer/Minden Pictures. 110-111 S Charlie Brown, 110b Michio Hoshino/Minden Pictures, 112-113 Norbert Wu/Minden Pictures, 112c Fritz Polking, 113b Fritz Polking. 114-115 Otto Plantema/Minden Pictures, 114c Yva Momatiuk, John Eastcott/Minden Pictures, 115b Jan Vermeer/Minden Pictures. 116-117 Panda Photo, 116b Bill Coster, 117t ImageBroker. 118-119 David Burton, 118c Marc Schwär/Imagebroker, 119c Bob Gibbons. 120-121 Norbert Wu/Minden Pictures, 120c Fred Bavendam/Minden Pictures, 121c Fred Bavendam/Minden Pictures. 122-123 Photo Researchers, 122bColin Marshall, 123t Jeff Rotman/Minden Pictures, 125t Colin Marshall, 125b Gerard Lacz. 126-127 Mike Parry/Minden Pictures, 127t ImageBroker. 128-129 Hiroya Minakuchi/Minden Pictures, 128b Jurgen and Christine Sohns, 129c Suzi Eszterhas/Minden Pictures. 130-131 Mike Parry/Minden Pictures, 130b Imagebroker, Norbert Probst, 132-133 Yva Momatiuk, John Eastcott/Minden Pictures, 132b Tui De Roy/Minden Pictures, 133b ÀBiosphoto , Sylvain Cordier/Biosphoto. 134-135 Patricio Robles Gil/Minden Pictures, 135c Cyril Ruoso/Minden Pictures, 135b Colin Marshall. 136-137 Kevin Schafer/Minden Pictures, 137t Helmut Corneli/Imagebroker, 137b Paul Hanna/Reuters. 138-139 Flip Nicklin/Minden Pictures, 139t Konrad Wothe/Minden Pictures, 139b R.Dirscherl.

GETTY

68b: G © Jeff Rotman, 89t Victoria Stone, Mark Deeble 50c: mongabay.com Dr. Hans Fricke 69t: Wikimedia Commons Canvasman21

NPL

87t David Shale, 124-125 Doug Perrine, 131t Doug Perrine

SCIENCE PHOTO LIBRARY 94-95 Christian Darkin

THE COMPLETE GUIDE TO
OCEAN
LIFE

CLAUDIA MARTIN

Sandy Creek
NEW YORK

CONTENTS

Words in **bold** are explained in the Glossary on page 140.

TAKE A DIP

If you were an alien looking down at our planet, you might wonder why it is called Earth. More than two-thirds of the world's surface is covered by ocean—not by earth.

FISHY FACT

We give the name sea to smaller areas of salty water that are partly surrounded by land. For example, the Caribbean Sea is part of the Atlantic Ocean.

The five oceans

Ocean is the name we give to the largest areas of salty water on our planet. There are five oceans. The Pacific Ocean is the largest: it covers 64 million square miles. The second largest is the Atlantic Ocean, which is followed by the Indian Ocean and then the Southern Ocean. The smallest ocean is the Arctic Ocean, at just 5 million square miles.

Arctic Ocean

Pacific Ocean

Atlantic Ocean

Indian Ocean

Southern Ocean

The continents divide the Earth's salty water into five oceans.

6

Why are the oceans salty?

The water in streams and lakes is not salty. We call it freshwater. But when this freshwater flows down rivers to the sea, it picks up salts from the rocks and soil. Over billions of years, the rivers have carried enough salt to the ocean to make it salty.

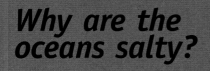

When rain falls onto the land, it forms lakes and streams. The water flows down rivers into the sea.

Warm and cold

The oceans are warm or cold depending on where they are in the world. Close to the equator, the oceans are warm and we call them **tropical**. Around the poles, the oceans are very cold and we call them polar. In between, we say that the oceans are temperate.

Warm water laps on the beaches of tropical islands

7

LIFE IN OUR OCEANS

There are at least 230,000 species of animals living in our oceans. But our oceans are so wide and deep that we are really only just starting to explore them. Scientists think that there may actually be ten times that number of species beneath the waves.

Fish often swim together with other fish of their species, like these bigeye and bluestripe snappers.

FISHY FACT

When an animal lives in the sea, we say that it is a *"marine"* animal.

A *life of challenges*

All ocean animals have had to adapt to the challenges of life underwater. First of all, every animal needs oxygen to survive, but there is very little oxygen in water. Then every animal must find food and escape its enemies. It must also adapt to its special habitat: whether that is the warmth of tropical seas or the cold of the poles, the breaking waves at the seashore or the dark of the deep ocean.

Mammals, such as the harp seal, have to go to the water's surface to breathe.

What's a species?

We divide the animal kingdom into groups. All the animals in a group share certain features, like having feathers, scales, or hair. There are six groups of animals: fish, invertebrates, mammals, reptiles, birds, and amphibians. Within these groups, scientists look for other similarities and differences between the animals and divide them into smaller and smaller groups. Eventually, they get to animals that look pretty much identical to each other. And all those animals are in the same **species**.

The great white shark is a species. It belongs to a family of large, fast-swimming sharks. This family is in the class of fish that all have skeletons made of cartilage.

FISH ANATOMY

FISHY FACT

Fish have a sixth sense—their lateral line system allows them to sense movement in the water.

More than 14,000 different species of fish live in the seas. All fish are covered in scales and have fins to help them swim. They breathe underwater using their **gills**. There are three types of fish: bony, cartilaginous, and jawless.

Gills

Just like us, fish need oxygen to survive. But unlike us, they can breathe underwater. Water contains a small amount of oxygen. Fish open their mouths and take in water. It is pumped to the gills, which are on either side of the fish's head. The gills absorb the oxygen in the water. The used water is then pumped out of the fish's body.

Most fish swim and steer with the help of dorsal fins (on the back), a pair of pectoral fins (on each side), a pair of pelvic fins and an anal fin (on the underside), and a tail fin.

10

Types of fish

The largest class of fish is the bony fish. These fish have hard skeletons made of bone. Sharks, rays, and skates make up the class of cartilaginous fish. They have skeletons made of softer cartilage. The group of jawless fish includes just the hagfish and lampreys. These strange creatures bore into their **prey** rather than bite it.

Along with sharks, sawfish are cartilaginous fish.

Unlike bony fish, sharks do not have covers over their gills. A tiger shark has five gill slits on either side.

INVERTEBRATE ANATOMY

An **invertebrate** is an animal without a backbone. Over 98 percent of animals are invertebrates. They live in the air, on land, in freshwater, and in the sea. The most common types of invertebrate in the sea are arthropods, mollusks, echinoderms, cnidarians, worms, and sponges.

Cnidarians

Cnidarians are very simple animals such as corals, sea anemones, sea fans, and jellyfish. They have stinging cells that they use for defense and capturing prey.

The Japanese spider crab is the world's largest crustacean, with a leg span of 12 feet.

Arthropods

Arthropods are the largest group of invertebrates. They have a hard external skeleton that protects their soft body. Insects, spiders, and **crustaceans** are all arthropods. Crustaceans include crabs, lobsters, shrimp, krill, and barnacles.

Mollusks

Mollusks have a soft body and a muscular feet or **tentacles**. Many of them have a shell. Common mollusks include snails, clams, mussels, octopuses, and squid.

The day octopus can swim at up to 25 miles per hour by shooting water out of its body. It is a mollusk.

FISHY FACT

The largest sea sponge is the monoraphus sponge, which can grow to 10 feet wide.

The red sea urchin is an echinoderm. It feeds on seaweeds, which it scrapes off the ocean floor.

Echinoderms

There are around 6,000 species of echinoderms. They have no head and their body is often divided into five or more parts. Most of them move around on tiny suckers called tubefeet. Starfish, sea cucumbers, and sea urchins are all echinoderms.

MAMMAL ANATOMY

FISHY FACT

The marine mammal most at risk of extinction is the vaquita porpoise: fewer than 300 are still alive.

Mammals share certain characteristics. Female mammals make milk to feed their young. All mammals have some hair on their bodies. There are 128 species of **marine** mammals. Since mammals need to breathe air into their lungs, marine mammals must return regularly to the water's surface.

Whales, dolphins, and porpoises

These animals are called cetaceans. They are so well adapted to life in the water that they hardly look like land mammals at all. They have one pair of flippers and powerful, flattened tails. They spend their entire lives at sea.

Seals, sea lions, and walruses

This group of mammals have sleek bodies and four wide flippers. They spend part of their lives on land, resting, breeding, and raising their young.

The world's smallest seal is the ringed seal, which lives in and around the Arctic.

The West Indian manatee is found in coastal waters, from the Caribbean to South America.

The harbor porpoise feeds on fish such as herring and mackerel

Manatees and dugongs

Manatees and dugongs are the only plant-eating marine mammals. Their two small flippers can be used like arms and they have a paddle-like tail. Just like the cetaceans, they never leave the sea.

Polar bears and sea otters

Three other mammals depend on the ocean for food: the polar bear and two species of otter. These animals have claws and thick fur to keep them warm.

The sea otter has the thickest fur of any animal

REPTILE ANATOMY

The easiest way to spot a **reptile** is by its skin, which is covered in tough scales. All reptiles are cold-blooded. This means that they need external sources of heat, such as the sun, to keep them warm. Most reptiles live on land, but a few species live in the sea. All sea-living reptiles must swim to the surface to breathe air into their lungs.

Crocodiles

Just two species of crocodiles live in the sea: the saltwater crocodile and the American crocodile. Crocodiles have powerful jaws lined with sharp teeth. They have strong bodies and tails, making them excellent swimmers. Like most reptiles, crocodiles lay eggs.

The American crocodile lives in freshwater and coastal seas from the southern USA to South America.

Turtles

There are eight species of sea turtle. Turtles have a bony shell that acts as a shield. They do not have teeth, so they chew food using their hard jaws. Sea turtles go ashore to lay their eggs on sandy beaches.

At 2–3 feet long, Kemp's Ridley sea turtle is the smallest sea turtle.

The marine iguana lives in the Galapagos Islands. It can dive over 30 feet into the water.

Lizards and snakes

Lizards and snakes form another group of reptiles. These reptiles can open their jaws very wide. Lots of snakes live in the sea, but only one sort of lizard does: the marine iguana. Like snakes found on land, sea snakes have no legs and are venomous.

BIRD ANATOMY

Birds are the only animals that are covered in feathers. They also have two legs and a pair of wings. Most birds use their wings to fly—but not all of them. All birds lay eggs that have hard shells.

FISHY FACT

Of the 10,000 species of birds, just a few hundred are seabirds.

What is a seabird?

Seabirds are birds that depend on the oceans for their food. Some seabirds fly over the vast oceans, trying to catch sight of fish or other sea creatures. Some seabirds are expert swimmers. One group of seabirds, the penguin, use their wings only for swimming and do not fly at all. All seabirds return to land to lay their eggs.

The Galapagos penguin is the only penguin that lives near the equator. Most penguins live in cooler regions.

Right for the job

The shape of a bird's feet tells us about where it lives. Most seabirds have webbed feet. These wide, flattened feet make good paddles for swimming. Birds that wade in soft mud and sand at the seashore have long, wide toes to stop them from sinking in. We can also discover how a bird feeds by looking at the size and shape of its beak. The brown pelican has a huge beak that allows it to snap up large fish. The pied avocet uses its thin, curved beak for poking in the mud and shallow water for tiny creatures.

The brown pelican uses its throat pouch as a basket for catching fish.

The pied avocet is often seen wading along muddy shorelines.

COLORFUL CORAL

Coral reefs are the beautiful, multicolored gardens of the sea. Reefs are very important **habitats** as they provide a home for the richest variety of life in the world's oceans. But our reefs are being put in danger by **global warming** and **pollution**.

Coral reefs provide a home for more than one million different types of animal.

A special habitat

Corals grow in many different colors and shapes, from fans to ferns to antlers to bubbles and brains. Tiny creatures called *zooxanthellae*, a sort of **algae**, grow on the coral. Other creatures, such as fish and starfish, come to feed on the algae and the coral itself. Yet larger creatures, from reef sharks to sea snakes, feed on these smaller animals.

Coral polyps have rows of tentacles surrounding their mouths

Brain coral feeds on small animals that drift past.

Growing coral

Coral reefs grow over thousands of years. They are built by tiny animals called coral polyps. These polyps make hard, bony skeletons around themselves for protection. When a polyp dies, another polyp settles on top of the skeleton. Together, thousands of polyps form a reef. Polyps can only grow in warm, shallow seawater.

STRIPES AND SPOTS

The fish that live on coral reefs are among the most colorful sea creatures of all. Some use their colors to **camouflage** themselves in the multicolored world of the reef. Others use bright stripes and spots to warn **predators** that they are unpleasant to eat. Some species use their patterns to find and attract a mate.

Copperband butterflyfish

This fish has a large, eye-like spot below the dorsal fin. The eye spot makes predators confused. Predators are likely to think that, with an eye this big, the fish is larger and stronger than it really is. If they do attack, predators will usually aim for a fish's tender eyes. By making attackers think that its tail is its head, the butterflyfish has bought itself a chance to escape.

The dark spot near the copperband butterflyfish's dorsal fin looks like a large eye.

The male mandarin dragonet attracts females by performing a dance to show off his beautiful patterns.

Predators may be frightened away by the clown triggerfish's bright yellow mouth.

Clown triggerfish

The clown triggerfish has large, white spots on the underside of its body. When the fish is seen from below, these spots make it blend into the dappled surface of the water. When seen from above, the yellow and black pattern on the fish's upper side helps it hide among the coral.

FISHY FACT

Even though coral reefs occupy only a tiny area of the world's oceans (just 1 percent), they provide a home for an amazing one-quarter of all marine fish species.

FIND A PARTNER

Some reef creatures develop partnerships with each other in order to survive. Sea anemones look like beautiful flowers, but they are actually animals that catch other creatures with their stinging tentacles. These fierce stings keep most reef fish away, but not the clever clown fish.

A special mucus covers the clown fish and protects it from the anemone's stings.

Clown fish

The clown fish is almost the only fish that is not harmed by the anemone's strong poison. Safe from its predators, the little fish finds shelter among the stinging tentacles. There it feeds on the scraps left over from the anemone's meals, such as small fish and shrimps. In return, the clown fish cleans the anemone's tentacles and eats up small animals that might harm the anemone.

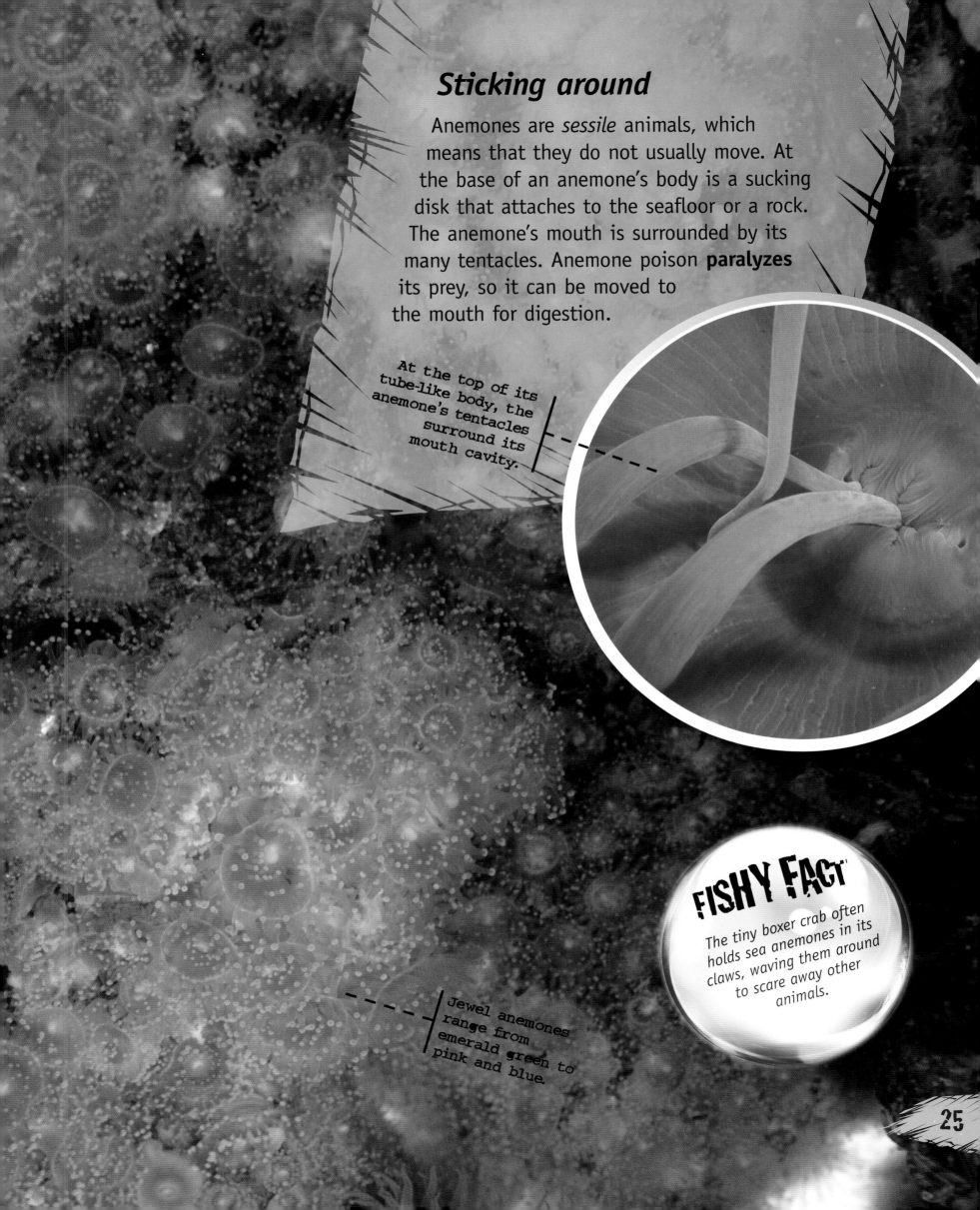

Sticking around

Anemones are *sessile* animals, which means that they do not usually move. At the base of an anemone's body is a sucking disk that attaches to the seafloor or a rock. The anemone's mouth is surrounded by its many tentacles. Anemone poison **paralyzes** its prey, so it can be moved to the mouth for digestion.

At the top of its tube-like body, the anemone's tentacles surround its mouth cavity.

Jewel anemones range from emerald green to pink and blue.

FISHY FACT

The tiny boxer crab often holds sea anemones in its claws, waving them around to scare away other animals.

ON THE DEFENSIVE

Reef creatures have developed some amazing strategies for defending themselves against predators. Of course, the simplest plan is to swim away and hide. Other animals use sharp spines, body armor, and some even stranger ideas.

Clever sea slugs

Sea slugs are a group of snails without shells. Aeolid sea slugs have a very cunning defense. As they munch on the tentacles of sea anemones, they keep the stinging cells for themselves, passing them into the spikes, or cerata, on their backs. Then the sea slugs use the anemone poison for their own protection.

As with many poisonous animals, the lionfish's bright stripes warn predators to keep well away.

An aeolid sea slug feeds on sea anemones, keeping the stings for its own use.

Spiny lionfish

The spiky striped lionfish has a deadly defensive weapon. The spines on its fins can give a poisonous sting. In fact, the **venom** is so strong that it is even dangerous to humans. The lionfish only uses this weapon to defend itself against predators, not to attack prey.

The honeycomb cowfish can change color to blend in with its surroundings.

Honeycomb cowfish

The honeycomb cowfish is almost completely covered in hard, plate-like scales. This armor prevents it from moving very fast, but few other fish are able to stomach eating it.

27

CLAMMING UP

A clam has a soft body that is protected within two hinged shells. The shells can be closed at the first sign of danger. Animals that live inside this sort of shell are called bivalves. The world's largest bivalve is the giant clam, which can grow up to 4.5 feet long and weigh as much as 660 pounds—that's as heavy as four men.

The flesh of the giant clam is a delicacy in some countries, but overfishing has led to the clam becoming endangered.

Sucking up

The giant clam fastens itself to a suitable spot on the reef using its foot. Once fixed, it will stay there for the rest of its life. The clam feeds using two tubes. The first tube sucks in water that contains small bits of food. The clam then filters, or strains, the food out of the water. The used water is pushed out through the second tube.

The giant clam's vivid colors come from the tiny, bright plants called zooxanthellae that live on its body.

Tall story

Pacific Islanders tell legends about giant clams that snap swimmers up in their shells, swallowing them whole. But no real giant clam deaths have ever been heard of. The muscles that the giant clam uses to close its shell move far too slowly to take anyone by surprise.

FISHY FACT

Fishermen in the Pacific Islands eat the giant clam's soft flesh, then keep the shell for bathing in.

CORAL CLEANERS

Unlike other crabs, the hermit crab does not have a shell of its own. It protects its soft body by living inside an empty seashell, which it carries around with it. Hermit crabs have an important job to do on the reef: they nibble on scraps of food they find. This keeps the coral clean and healthy.

A hermit crab carries its "mobile home" around with it.

Moving house

The abandoned shells of sea snails are popular homes for hermit crabs. But sometimes crabs use a clam or mussel shell— or even a hollow piece of wood or stone. The important thing is that the shell is the right size to protect the crab and still leave it room to grow. When it grows too big for its shell, a hermit crab must hunt for another.

A hermit crab's eyes are on stalks, while its antennae are used for touch and to sense chemicals in the water.

Sometimes there are not enough empty shells to go around, so hermit crabs fight for the best ones.

Form a line

When a new, bigger shell is found, a group of hermit crabs will sometimes form a line. The largest crab will go at the front, and the smallest at the back. As the largest snail moves into the new shell, the next crab in the line will move into that crab's old shell. This carries on down the line until every crab has a new home.

WORMS IN THE WATER

Worms don't only live in the earth. Some live in our oceans. Sea worms have a long, tube-like body and no legs. They are invertebrates, which means that they do not have a backbone.

The racing-stripe flatworm lives on coral reefs in the Pacific Ocean.

Racing stripe flatworm

The flatworms are named for their long, flattened bodies. Many flatworms are brightly colored, which lets predators know that they taste horrible. The racing stripe flatworm has a white stripe down its purple body.

Feather duster worm

A feather duster worm attaches itself to the reef or seabed and builds a hard tube around its body for protection. The tube is made of sand and bits of shell stuck together with a gluey mucus made in the worm's body. The worm catches food with its sticky, feathery tentacles. If it senses danger, the worm slides back into its tube.

FISHY FACT

The longest animal in the world is probably the bootlace worm. It can grow to a whopping 180 feet long.

A feather duster worm's crown of tentacles is very sensitive to light, touch, and motion in the water.

Christmas tree worm

The Christmas tree worm has colorful spiral gills that look a bit like a Christmas tree. The gills allow the worm to breathe and also catch small bits of food that come drifting by.

A Christmas tree worm's spiral-shaped gills range from yellow to purple and pink.

GREEN TURTLES

The green turtle has scaly, waterproof skin and a tough shell. It is often found swimming in shallow water near to coasts, among seagrass or coral reefs. Like all marine reptiles, the green turtle must come on land to lay its eggs.

Egg laying

Every year, female turtles swim great distances—perhaps over a thousand miles—to return to the beach where they were born. This is where they will lay their own eggs. Each turtle digs a hole in the sand using her flippers. She then lays her eggs in the nest, covers them carefully with sand, and returns to the sea. Around two months later, the newborn turtles dig their way out of the sand and start to make their way to the water. This is a dangerous time. Predators such as gulls and crabs are waiting for the tiny turtles. Not all of them will make it to the sea.

A female green turtle lays 100 to 200 eggs in a burrow that she digs in the sand.

A green turtle can live for up to 80 years in the wild

Strong swimmer

With their paddle-like flippers and flattened bodies, green turtles are expert swimmers. Their beaks have serrated edges, like the teeth of a saw. This allows them to tear seagrass to eat, and scrape algae such as seaweed off hard surfaces.

Hatchlings make their way straight to the sea using their sense of smell.

THE OPEN OCEAN

The wide oceans, far from land, are home to an amazing range of sea creatures, from tiny plankton to giant whales. Animals living in the open sea have nowhere to hide, so they must find different ways to stay safe. Some are very fast swimmers while others can give electric shocks or poisonous stings. Some of the ocean's most powerful predators live in the open ocean.

Young barracuda find safety in numbers by moving in a large shoal.

Striped dolphins swim far from land, where they leap and play in the surface waters.

At night, the Humboldt squid travels to the surface waters to hunt for prey.

Zones of the sea

Scientists divide the ocean world into different zones, depending on depth. Near the surface of the ocean, the water is lit by sunshine. This is the sunlit zone. The sunlight gives life to green plants, which are food for many animals. The sunlit zone is filled with life. The sea creatures that we know most about live in this zone, from dolphins and whales to an enormous number of different fish.

As you dive deeper into the ocean, you move into the twilight zone. The water here is darker and colder. In this zone, many fish and squid make their own light. Some creatures travel up to the busier surface waters when they want to hunt for food. Deeper still lie the so-called midnight zone, the abyss, and the trenches.

PRECIOUS PLANKTON

If you looked at a drop of seawater under a microscope you would be amazed to see tiny plants and animals. These are called **plankton**. In one way or another, plankton provide the food for almost every sea creature.

Billions of tiny animals known as zooplankton, such as this copepod, drift in the world's oceans.

The food chain

Tiny plants called phytoplankton drift in the sunlit surface waters of the ocean. Like other plants, they use the sunlight to make food for themselves. These plant plankton are eaten by tiny, drifting ocean animals, called animal plankton or zooplankton. The zooplankton are eaten by small fish. The small fish are eaten by larger sea creatures. This is called a food chain. Even deep-sea creatures are part of the chain, as they feed on dead plants and animals that sink to the ocean floor.

One of the ocean's largest creatures, the bowhead whale feeds on zooplankton.

Diatoms are one of the most common types of plant plankton. They can only be seen under a microscope.

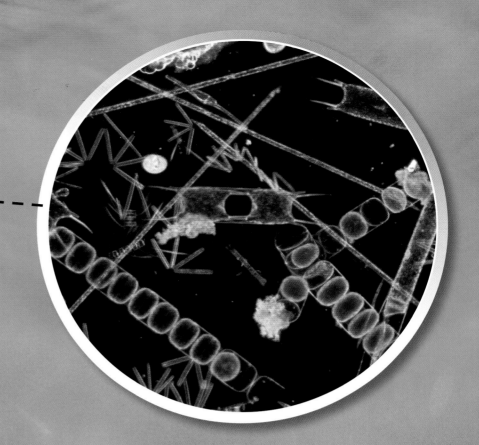

Drifters

The word plankton means drifter. Plankton include any sea creature that just drifts on the current, without moving itself by swimming or pushing through the water. Most animal plankton are so small that it cannot be seen without a microscope. But some animal plankton, such as floating jellyfish, are large. Not all animal plankton stay as plankton for their whole life. Plankton also include the eggs and larvae (young) of animals such as fish and crabs.

FISHY FACT
When conditions are right, so much greenish plant plankton grow in the water that it can be seen from space as a giant "plankton bloom."

FASTEST FISH

Some large fish are high-speed swimmers. They are able to swim great distances very fast in order to catch their prey. The fastest fish of all is the sailfish, which has been recorded swimming at an astonishing 68 miles per hour.

After a sudden burst of speed, the sailfish sometimes raises its sail. This helps it to cool down.

Speedy sailfish

The sailfish has a sleek, **streamlined** body, which lets it cut through the water at great speed. Its tall dorsal fin looks like a sail, but it is kept folded down when swimming. The sail is raised when the fish is in danger or gets excited. This allows the sailfish to seem bigger than it really is. Groups of sailfish sometimes raise their sails when they are cornering a shoal of fish in order to feed on them.

Mighty marlin

Marlin have long bodies and spear-like snouts. These spears can injure or kill when a marlin shoots through a shoal of fish at top speed. The marlin then returns to eat its prize. Marlins are the only fish to reach speeds rivaling the extraordinary sailfish.

The Atlantic blue marlin grows up to 13 feet long.

Talented tuna

Tuna probably win third prize when it comes to speed, clocking up a pace of 50 miles per hour. All 13 species of tuna are expert hunters, feeding on fish and squid.

A Pacific bluefin tuna hunts sardines.

FLYING FISH

The flying fish can leap right out of the water and glide through the air. This is a perfect way to escape from their predators, which include fast swimmers like dolphins, tuna, and marlin. Flying fish have unusually large pectoral fins on their sides. These work like a pair of wings!

Taking to the air

There are around 40 species of flying fish living in the warm and tropical regions of the oceans. The flying fish's streamlined shape allows it to pick up great speed underwater, reaching 37 miles per hour. As it breaks the surface of the water, the flying fish's wing-like fins lift it into the air while its quickly beating tail pushes it forward.

To push out of the water, a flying fish beats its tail 70 times per second.

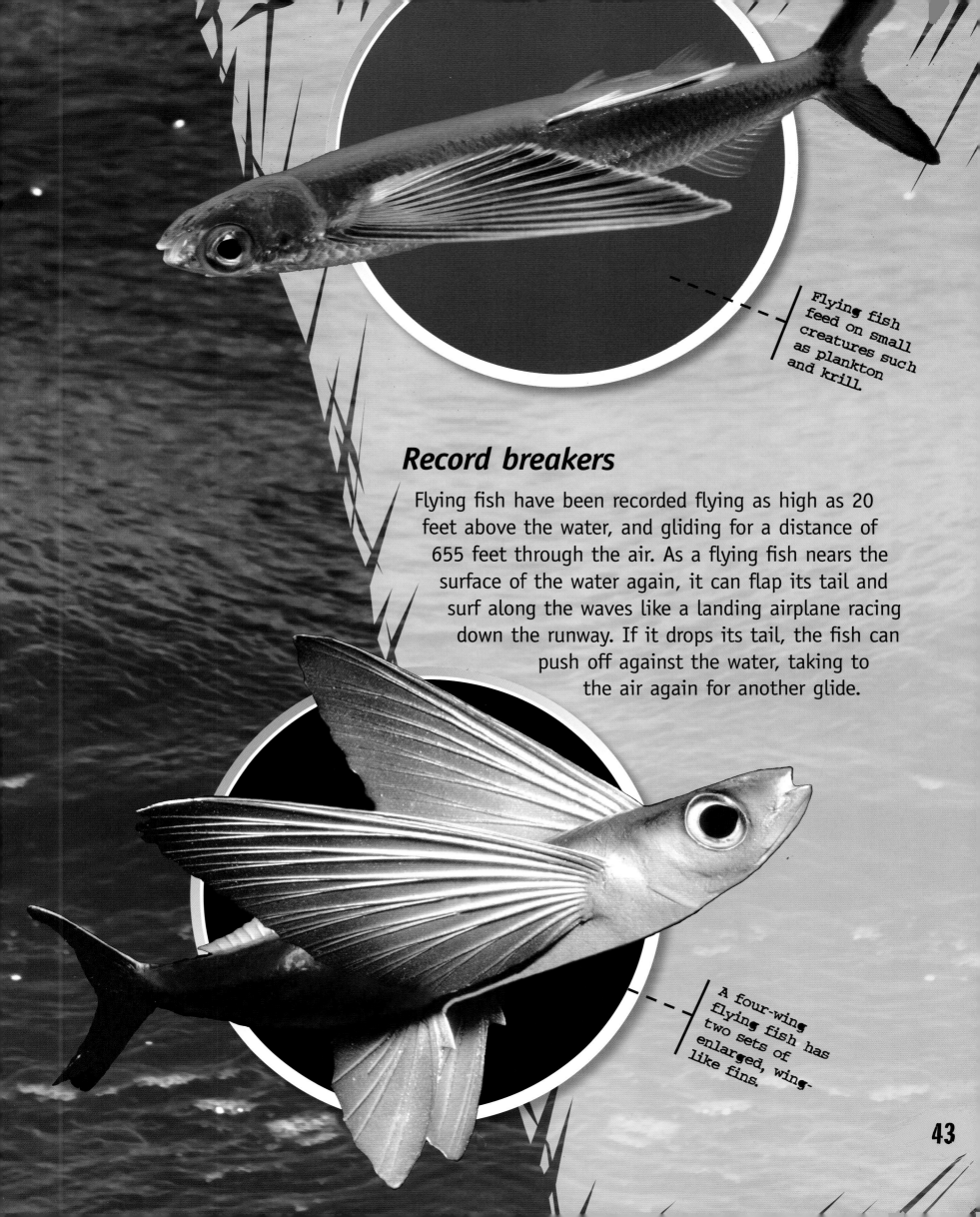

Flying fish
feed on small
creatures such
as plankton
and krill.

Record breakers

Flying fish have been recorded flying as high as 20
feet above the water, and gliding for a distance of
655 feet through the air. As a flying fish nears the
surface of the water again, it can flap its tail and
surf along the waves like a landing airplane racing
down the runway. If it drops its tail, the fish can
push off against the water, taking to
the air again for another glide.

A four-wing
flying fish has
two sets of
enlarged, wing-
like fins.

FOOD FISH

Every year, more than 2 trillion fish are caught from the oceans and make their way to our fish markets, shops—and eventually our plates! Millions of people rely on fishing for their livelihoods. The species of fish most often caught to eat include herring, cod, anchovy, tuna, flounder, and mullet.

The silver of the sea

For centuries, fishing for herring has been so important to fishermen of many countries that these fish have been called "the silver of the sea." Herring often move in large **schools** close to coasts, which makes them easy to catch in giant nets.

Sockeye salmon are caught in a net in Kamchatka, Russia, Pacific Ocean.

Tasty anchovies

Anchovies are small green-blue fish. They are common in the Atlantic, Indian, and Pacific Oceans. The strong flavor of anchovies makes them a favorite with humans. Anchovies are often salted and packed in cans.

There are more than 4 million fishing boats in the world, ranging from rowing boats to huge trawlers.

Cod at risk

Atlantic cod is a very popular food fish because of its tasty flesh. In fact, it is so popular that we have eaten too many of them. If too many fish from one species are caught, the fish population never recovers. This is called overfishing. Fishermen are now given limits on the number of cod they can catch.

The Atlantic cod has a sensitive barbel on its chin, which helps it search for food.

FLATFISH

Flatfish are quite simply—flat! They spend most of their lives lying on the ocean floor, where they go unnoticed among the sand, mud, or pebbles. When some suitable prey, such as a smaller fish, swims past, the flatfish takes it by surprise.

A flounder lies camouflaged on the seafloor, hidden from its enemies and waiting for its prey.

Most species of turbot have their eyes on the left side of their body.

Looking up

Young flatfish have rounded bodies, but they flatten as they grow. At the same time, the eye on one side of the body moves slowly around so that both eyes lie on one side. Some species have both eyes on their left side, while others have them on their right. When a flatfish lies on the ocean floor, its eyes face upward.

A black-tip sole can use its eyes as a periscope that rotates 180 degrees.

Camouflage

Many flatfish are camouflaged so that they are almost invisible on the ocean floor. The upper side of the turbot is speckled so that it blends into the sandy or pebbly seabed. Flounders can change their color and pattern to match whatever sea bottom they are on. On sand they are pale and blotchy, while on mud they are brown and mottled. Many flatfish, such as sole, half-bury themselves in the sand or mud, ready to ambush their prey.

FISHY FACT

The peacock flounder can change its color to match its surroundings in just 8 seconds.

STRANGE SUNFISH

The ocean sunfish must win the award for the oddest-looking fish. It looks like it has lost its tail! Instead of having a tail fin, the sunfish's body is rounded at the back. The fish is also strangely flattened, so that it is very thin when seen head on.

Sunfish often swim among seaweed called kelp, where there are plenty of smaller fish to nibble the parasites off their skin.

FISHY FACT

Sunfish prefer to eat jellyfish. Many die after eating plastic bags, which look like jellyfish floating in the water.

Sunbathing

Sunfish are usually found in warmer water, where they are often seen floating on their sides at the surface. Scientists think that the sunfish are warming themselves in the sunshine after a dive into deeper, colder water.

The ocean sunfish swings its long dorsal (top) and anal (bottom) fins like oars to move through the water.

What a whopper

The sunfish is one of the largest fish in the ocean. It can reach 14 feet tall from the tip of the dorsal fin to the bottom of the anal fin. Fish weighing as much as 5,100 pounds have been recorded—that's as heavy as 30 men!

Is it a shark?

Since the sunfish has no tail fin and very small side fins, it swims and steers using the huge fins at the top and bottom of its body. Its tall dorsal fin sometimes creates panic when it is mistaken for a shark's fin above the water.

The sunfish's name comes from its habit of sunbathing at the ocean surface.

THE COELACANTH

In 1938, a truly amazing fish was caught off the coast of South Africa. What was so amazing about it was that everyone thought this fish had been extinct for millions of years. The fish was called the coelacanth.

Coelacanths have thick scales that act as body armor to protect them from predators.

Cave dweller

We know about two species of coelacanth, which both live in the Indian Ocean. During the daytime, the coelacanth hides in an underwater cave. At night, it drifts slowly in the ocean currents to find smaller fish to feed on. Its huge eyes are excellent at seeing in darkened caves and the night-time ocean.

Living fossil

Fossils are the remains of animals or plants that lived long ago. The coelacanth is known as a "living fossil" because it looks just like the coelacanth fossils that have been found from millions of years ago. This is unusual because most animals change, or evolve, over time. But the coelacanth still looks like it did when dinosaurs walked the earth, long before the first human beings.

This is a fossil of a coelacanth that lived about 150 million years ago.

51

FISH FATHERS

Unlike mammals, such as humans or whales, fish do not usually take care of their young. For most fish, after the mother has laid the eggs and the father has fertilized them, the eggs are left on their own. But some fish are quite different. Not only are the eggs cared for by a parent, but that parent is the father.

A male garibaldi works hard to tidy his nest, carrying away loose vegetation and any stray sea stars or urchins.

Egg carriers

Some species of fish rely on the male to hold onto the eggs until they hatch, keeping them safe from predators. Male nurseryfish carry their eggs on hooks on their foreheads. Hardhead catfish eggs are collected by the male and held in his mouth for a month until they hatch. He cannot feed for all this time.

FISHY FACT

It is very unusual for female sea fish to take care of their eggs, but the Antarctic plunderfish does. The mother builds a nest and guards her eggs for up to five months.

Banggai
cardinalfish
fathers hold
their eggs in
their mouths.

Nest guarding

A male stickleback builds a nest from vegetation and then sets about attracting a female. The female lays her eggs inside the nest and the male fertilizes them. He then guards them until they hatch. Male garibaldis are also nest builders. While he waits for his eggs to hatch, the garibaldi will attack any fish, and even humans, if they come too close.

A male stickleback fans
water over his nest
with his tail, making
sure the eggs get
enough oxygen.

JAW DROPPERS

Hagfish and lampreys are fish-like animals that share the very strange feature of not having a jaw. Hagfish look like eels and are well known for making slime. Lampreys, which are also eel-like, have a sucking mouth. Scientists have debated which group of animals these jaw-less creatures belong to.

FISHY FACT

If they are captured, hagfish get free by tying themselves in a knot that works itself down from the head to the tail.

A sea lamprey's mouth works like a suction cup.

Blood-sucker

The sea lamprey feeds on blood. It attaches itself to a fish with its sucking mouth. The lamprey uses its teeth and sharp tongue to cut through the fish's flesh until it reaches blood. Then it begins to suck. A special substance in the lamprey's mouth stops its prey's blood from clotting and keeps it flowing. The prey slowly dies from blood loss.

Slimy hagfish

Hagfish don't have a jaw to bite with, but they do have a toothed tongue that they use to rip at their prey. Hagfish often bore into the bodies of dead or injured sea creatures, ripping out their insides to eat first. When they are in danger, hagfish create slime, which makes them too slippery for predators to hold onto.

The Pacific hagfish has feelers beside its mouth to help it find food on the seafloor.

When frightened, a hagfish's skin oozes mucus, which turns into a cloud of slime in the water.

CLEVER CAMOUFLAGE

Camouflage is the way an animal blends in with its surroundings so that it is not noticed. Camouflage allows predators to creep up on their prey, and prey animals to hide from their predators. Many sea creatures use camouflage, but some are masters of the art.

Blending in

The crocodilefish lies flat on the sandy seabed, where its blotchy brown, green, and gray pattern makes it nearly invisible. Its relative, the stonefish, uses its brown and gray markings to hide among stones, waiting for a tasty shrimp to come by.

FISHY FACT

The long, thin trumpetfish often swims vertically to hide among fronds of soft coral such as sea pens.

The crocodilefish has flaps called lappets over its eyes to keep them hidden.

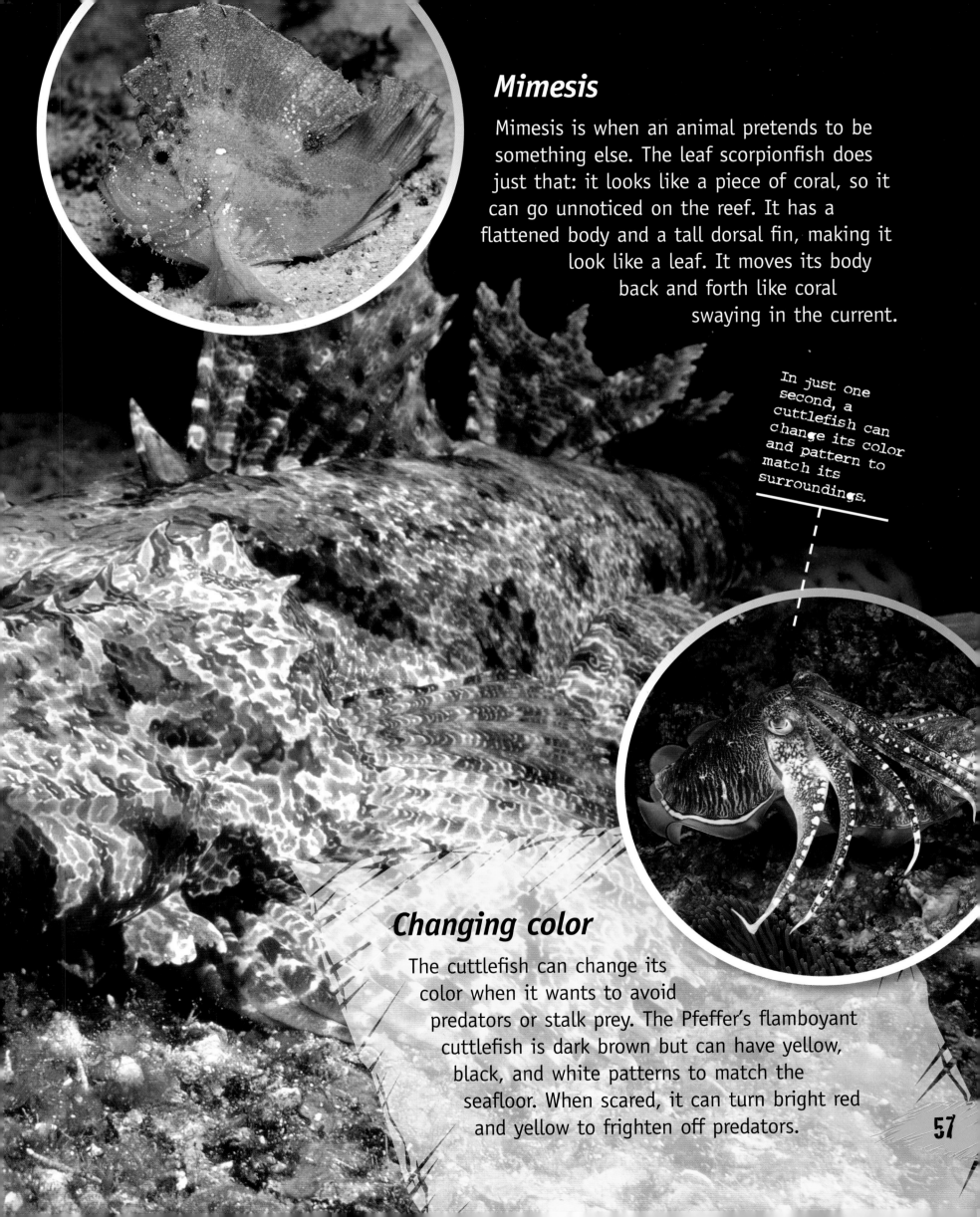

Mimesis

Mimesis is when an animal pretends to be something else. The leaf scorpionfish does just that: it looks like a piece of coral, so it can go unnoticed on the reef. It has a flattened body and a tall dorsal fin, making it look like a leaf. It moves its body back and forth like coral swaying in the current.

In just one second, a cuttlefish can change its color and pattern to match its surroundings.

Changing color

The cuttlefish can change its color when it wants to avoid predators or stalk prey. The Pfeffer's flamboyant cuttlefish is dark brown but can have yellow, black, and white patterns to match the seafloor. When scared, it can turn bright red and yellow to frighten off predators.

57

ALL PUFFED UP

Pufferfish, porcupinefish, balloonfish, and blowfish all share a clever way of defending themselves against predators. They can puff themselves up to two or three times their normal size, making them a very difficult snack to swallow.

A scared porcupinefish can double its body size.

Porcupinefish

Long, sharp spines cover the whole body of the porcupinefish. As with its relative the pufferfish, these spines lie flat until the porcupinefish swallows water to inflate itself. Porcupinefish are also highly poisonous. In fact, these slow-swimming fish are so good at defending themselves that they are preyed on only by huge sharks and orcas. Porcupinefish themselves prey on shellfish and crabs, using their sharp beak-like teeth to crush the shells.

Oceanic pufferfish

This pufferfish has quite a normal body shape for a fish—until it feels threatened, when it swallows enough water to inflate itself into a ball. When the fish is inflated, small spines on its belly stand upright, making it very prickly. As a third defense, the oceanic pufferfish is the most poisonous fish in the world. Even humans risk being killed by its venom if they eat it.

The pufferfish's stomach is very stretchy and it has no ribs, so it can gulp down water to inflate like a ball.

When calm, the pufferfish has a stout body that slims down toward its tail.

FISHY FACT

The porcupinefish makes a poison that is more than 1,000 times stronger than cyanide, the favorite poison of many murderers.

MANTA RAYS

The giant oceanic manta ray is the largest of the rays and one of the world's biggest fish. It can grow to 25 feet across and weigh up to 5,300 lb—that's about as heavy as a car! The manta ray appears to fly through the water by flapping its huge wing-like fins.

FISHY FACT

Manta rays sometimes leap right out of the water, maybe to communicate with other rays and maybe just because it's a fun thing to do!

Cleaning up

Manta rays often visit cleaning stations, places where animals such as large fish or turtles regularly come to be cleaned. At a station, little angelfish or wrasse swim over the manta's skin and gills. They nibble away the uncomfortable dead skin and **parasites**, while getting a good meal in the process.

Gentle giant

Despite its great size, the oceanic manta ray is not a terrifying predator. As seawater flows into its open mouth, the ray strains the tiny animal plankton out of the water. The flaps on either side of the ray's mouth help to funnel the seawater inside. When the ray is not feeding, it closes the flaps across its mouth.

A manta ray is being cleaned.

A fish called the remora often attaches itself to a manta ray and catches food that falls from its mouth.

ARMED AND DANGEROUS

There are 300 different species of shark, from the tiny dwarf lanternshark to the short-fin mako shark, the fastest of all sharks. With their keen senses of smell, sight, and hearing, many sharks are powerful hunters. Sharks are cartilaginous fish, which means that they have skeletons made of soft cartilage rather than bone.

The sharp, strong teeth of a bull shark are perfect for biting into fish, turtles, dolphins, and other bull sharks.

Shark teeth

The teeth of each shark are shaped to help it catch and eat its prey. Horn sharks have sharp teeth at the front of their jaws to catch small fish, and flat teeth at the back to crush shellfish. The mako shark catches slippery fish, so its teeth are long, thin, and pointed.

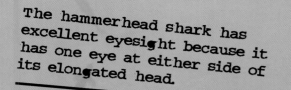
The hammerhead shark has excellent eyesight because it has one eye at either side of its elongated head.

Streamlined skin

Sharks don't just have teeth in their mouths. Shark skin is covered by very tiny teeth. These teeth point backward and help to guide water over the shark's body so that it can cut swiftly through the ocean.

Keep on moving

Just like other fish, sharks need to take in oxygen from the water through their gills. Many species of sharks must always keep swimming in order to move the oxygen-rich water over their gills. If they stop, they drown.

63

SHARK ATTACK

Some large sharks—such as the great white, bull, and oceanic whitetip—are among the fiercest hunters in our oceans. With their wickedly sharp teeth, these powerful predators are not afraid to attack any animal they come across. But do they really attack people?

The great white shark ambushes its prey, taking it by surprise from below.

The great white shark

The great white shark has attacked more people than any other species of sharks. This huge fish has been known to grow to over 20 feet and has teeth 3 inches long. But the great white shark prefers to feed on fish, dolphins, seals, and turtles rather than people.

Just a little taste

Everyone's heard scary stories about sharks attacking people. The truth is that every year about 60 people around the world are attacked by sharks. But don't worry too much: shark attacks are not usually fatal! Scientists think that sharks don't attack people in order to eat them—humans are just not meaty enough for them. When a shark bites a surfer or swimmer, it is probably just trying to find out what this strange animal is. After all, a shark doesn't have hands or feet to touch them with. After one bite, the shark will probably swim away.

Despite the oceanic tiger shark's vicious reputation, divers sometimes risk getting up close.

BIGGEST FISH

The biggest fish in the world is a whale shark. It can grown up to 41 feet long. But this giant isn't a terrifying hunter like the great white shark. It feeds on tiny plankton.

The whale shark can suck and gulp food-filled water into its mouth.

Basking sharks feed close to the surface of the water.

Filtered water is pushed out through the whale shark's ten gills.

Basking shark

The second biggest fish in the world is also a shark: the basking shark. The largest ever measured was 40 feet long. Just like the whale shark, the basking shark feeds by filtering plankton and other small creatures out of the water. It may travel thousands of miles every year, searching for plankton blooms, where huge amounts of plankton grow in the water.

Whale shark

This shark feeds by opening its huge mouth—which can be up to 5 feet wide—as it swims through the water. Water filled with algae, krill, larvae, and small squid flows into its mouth. Ten filter pads in the whale shark's mouth strain the food out of the water, which then runs out through the gills.

FISHY FACT

Basking sharks give birth to live young, which are already 5–6.5 feet long.

ELECTRIC SHOCK

Here's a shocking fact—some sea creatures can make their own electricity! Their special electricity-making organs help them stun their prey and keep away predators. The top three electricity producers are electric rays, electric stargazers, and skates.

Electric rays

These flat-looking fish can create electric shocks of up to 220 volts. That's enough to kill a fish, and even to throw a grown man to the ground. These rays often hide in the sand on the ocean floor, waiting for fish and other small creatures to stun.

An electric ray has an electricity-making organ on each side of its head.

FISHY FACT

The weapon known as the torpedo, which is fired at underwater targets, was named after the electric torpedo rays.

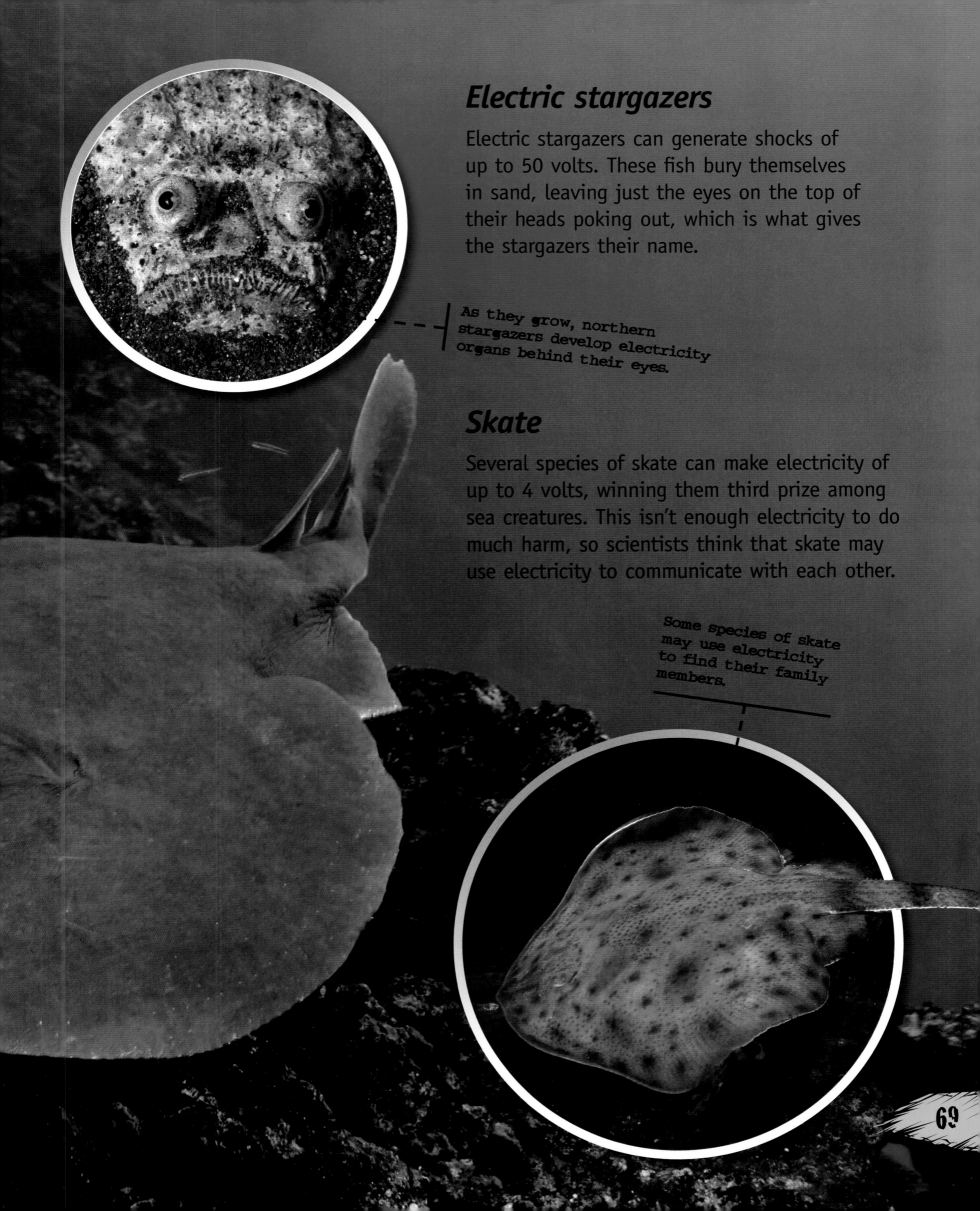

Electric stargazers

Electric stargazers can generate shocks of up to 50 volts. These fish bury themselves in sand, leaving just the eyes on the top of their heads poking out, which is what gives the stargazers their name.

As they grow, northern stargazers develop electricity organs behind their eyes.

Skate

Several species of skate can make electricity of up to 4 volts, winning them third prize among sea creatures. This isn't enough electricity to do much harm, so scientists think that skate may use electricity to communicate with each other.

Some species of skate may use electricity to find their family members.

INCREDIBLE JOURNEYS

Many ocean animals migrate, traveling from one place to another. Some migrations are short and happen every day, as when fish and squid swim up from the ocean depths to feed near the surface at night. Other migrations are incredibly long and happen just once a year, as animals travel from one side of the world to the other.

A Pacific leatherback turtle lays her eggs on a sandy beach in Indonesia.

Gray whale

Of all the mammals, the gray whale makes the longest journey. These whales swim 14,000 miles between their feeding grounds in the Arctic and the coast of California, where they breed.

During its migration, the gray whale travels at around 75 miles a day.

70

Arctic tern

The longest migration of any animal is made by a seabird called the Arctic tern. It flies over 44,000 miles a year as it journeys between the Arctic and Antarctic and back again. It does this to make the most of the short summer season at each pole.

The Arctic tern nests in the Arctic but migrates each year to the Antarctic Ocean.

Leatherback turtle

The Pacific leatherback turtle probably makes the longest migration of all reptiles. Every year it swims 12,000 miles across the Pacific Ocean and back. This takes it between the beaches where it nests in Indonesia and the coast of California, where it likes to eat jellyfish.

BLUE-RINGED OCTOPUS

The blue-ring is 4–8 inches long and lives in tropical areas of the Pacific and Indian Oceans.

The blue-ringed octopus is small, but its venom is deadly enough to kill humans. Like all octopuses, the blue-ringed octopus has eight arms. It has no skeleton, so it is bendy enough to squeeze into tight holes in rocks and hide from its enemies.

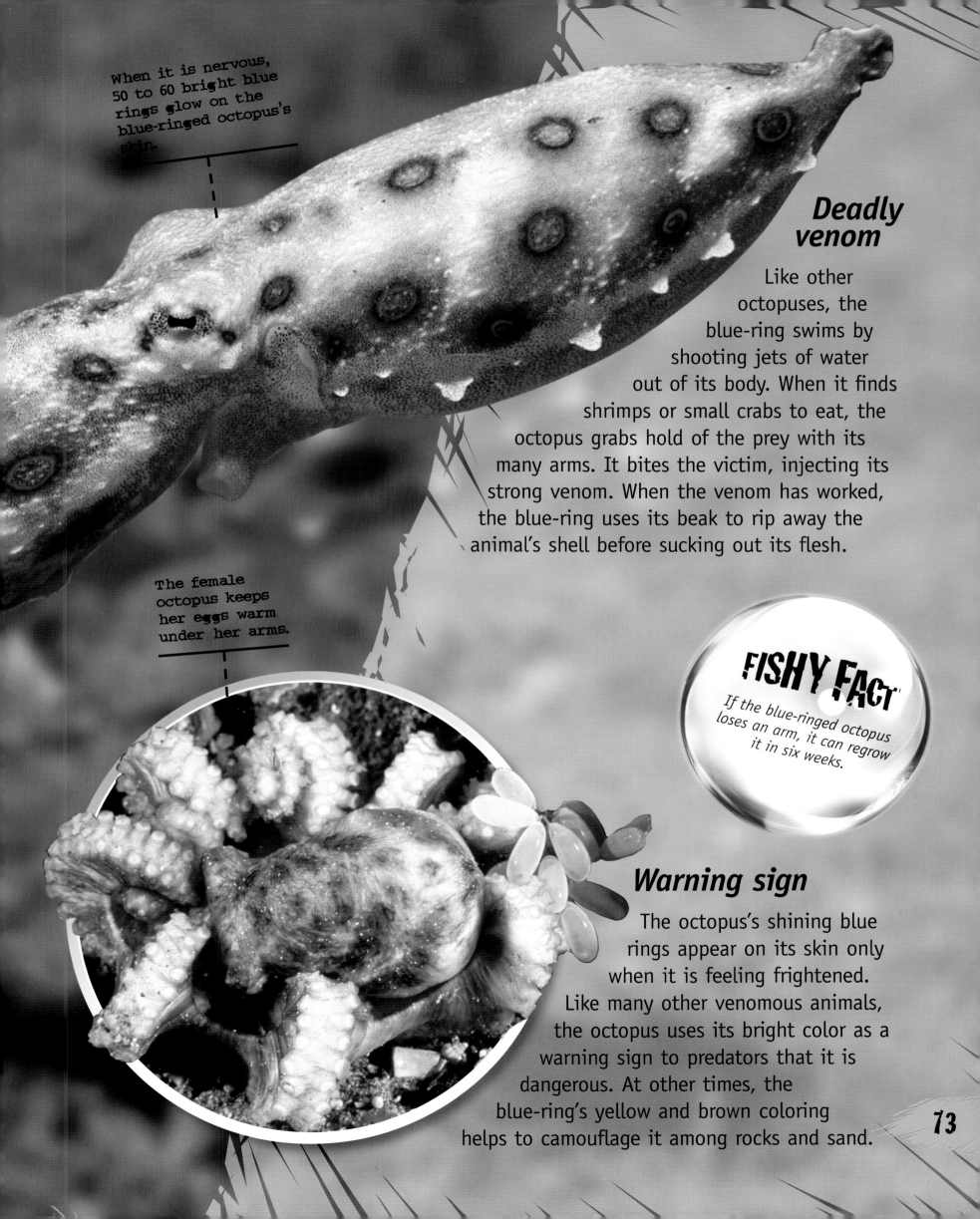

When it is nervous, 50 to 60 bright blue rings glow on the blue-ringed octopus's skin.

The female octopus keeps her eggs warm under her arms.

Deadly venom

Like other octopuses, the blue-ring swims by shooting jets of water out of its body. When it finds shrimps or small crabs to eat, the octopus grabs hold of the prey with its many arms. It bites the victim, injecting its strong venom. When the venom has worked, the blue-ring uses its beak to rip away the animal's shell before sucking out its flesh.

FISHY FACT

If the blue-ringed octopus loses an arm, it can regrow it in six weeks.

Warning sign

The octopus's shining blue rings appear on its skin only when it is feeling frightened. Like many other venomous animals, the octopus uses its bright color as a warning sign to predators that it is dangerous. At other times, the blue-ring's yellow and brown coloring helps to camouflage it among rocks and sand.

73

STINGING JELLYFISH

Despite its name, a jellyfish is not a fish. It is an invertebrate, which is an animal without a backbone. A jellyfish has a squashy umbrella-shaped body. Its tentacles are covered with venomous stingers, which it uses to catch prey. Every year, thousands of unlucky people are stung by jellyfish at the seaside.

Lion's mane jellyfish

The largest jellyfish in the world is probably the lion's mane. The biggest ever found had a body 7 feet 6 inches wide. Its trailing tentacles were a mind-boggling 120 feet long. This jellyfish lives for just one year.

The lion's mane jellyfish captures zooplankton, small fish, and other jellyfish with its tentacles.

Sea wasp

The sea wasp jellyfish is one of the deadliest in the world. Its pale blue body is see-through, which makes it hard to spot in the water. The amount of venom in just one sea wasp is enough to kill 60 grown men. If untreated, a victim can die in three minutes.

Luckily, hospitals near where the jellyfish lives keep an **antivenom** to treat stings. You might like to remember that the sea wasp is found around the coasts of northern Australia and southeast Asia!

FISHY FACT

Jellyfish often drift on the ocean currents in groups of hundreds or thousand. These groups can be called blooms, swarms, or smacks.

Flower hat jellyfish have a see-through body with dark stripes.

75

LIVING IN A POD

Whales are the largest of the mammals that live in the ocean. Like all mammals, whales need to breathe air using their lungs. This means that, although they can dive deep into the sea, they must return to the surface to breathe. Whales feed their young on milk, just like other mammals.

When a whale breathes out, the wet "blow" can spout high in the air.

Whale mothers usually give birth to one calf at a time. It stays close to her side for up to a year.

FISHY FACT
Some species of whales are well known for floating on the water surface for short periods: they are taking a nap!

Friendly whales

Whales enjoy living in the company of other whales.
They usually move in groups called pods, finding
food and taking care of their young together.
Some whales show signs of forming particular
friendships with each other. Scientists study
the way whales communicate using different
sounds, touch, and movements.

Southern right
whales are
great acrobats
and often leap,
or breach, out
of the water.

Leaping
and playing

If you ever go on a whale-
watching trip you will be amazed
to see whales leaping out of the
water then crashing down with a huge
splash. This is called breaching. We don't
know for sure why whales do it.
Sometimes they may be defending
themselves or herding their prey. Sometimes
they seem to be playing. Whales also slap their
flippers and tails on the water. A male might do
this to warn off a rival. At other times, we're
pretty sure they just find it fun.

HUMPBACK WHALES

The wiry baleen plates around the humpback's mouth are perfect for trapping food.

The humpback whale has a stocky body, knobbly head, and huge flippers. It often plays at the water's surface, leaping, slapping its tail—and even lying on its back waving its flippers in the air. The humpback is also well known for its songs.

Singing whales

Male humpbacks sing the longest and most complex songs of any animal, apart from humans. When it is time to find a mate, the males hang in the water with their heads down and sing to the females. Their songs are made up of patterns of squeals, whistles, grunts, and wails. A song may last a full half hour. When they have paused for breath, the whales may sing the same song again.

Blowing bubbles

A humpback has hundreds of bristly plates, known as baleen, hanging from its upper jaw. These plates are used to strain food such as fish and krill out of the water. Sometimes groups of humpbacks work together to capture their prey. They all swim around a school of fish while blowing bubbles from their blowholes. This forces the fish into a tightly packed ball. Then the whales swoop on the fish together.

A humpback raises its tail high in the air before diving.

Humpback whales move in family groups of three or four, but come together in much larger numbers at feeding areas.

FISHY FACT

Humpback whales can grow to 52 feet long and weigh 79,000 pounds—which is as heavy as 10 African elephants.

BOTTLENOSE DOLPHINS

Bottlenose dolphins can leap high out of the water, performing spins and somersaults.

The curved mouth of this dolphin makes it look as if it is smiling. Its brain is about half the size of a human's, but the bottlenose is still a very clever animal. It is such a good learner that it is often taught to perform tricks in aquariums. Although if it were really clever, perhaps it would refuse to do them!

Hearing echoes

The bottlenose is the most common of the ocean dolphins. Dolphins are actually small, toothed whales. They have slim, sleek bodies so that they can swim fast through the water. Dolphins also have an amazing ability called echolocation. They send out a stream of clicks and listen for the echoes to come back. The time that it takes for the echoes to return tells dolphins all about the shape, size, and movement of the objects around them. This makes them expert hunters.

Several mothers and their young dolphins normally live together in a group.

Despite its smiling face, a bottlenose dolphin can be fierce when it needs to defend itself.

Using tools

Some groups of bottlenose dolphins are so clever that they can use tools. In Shark Bay in Australia, female bottlenoses place sea sponges on their beaks when they search for food on the seabed. It seems that mother dolphins teach this skill to their daughters so that they don't hurt themselves when they look for food on the rough ocean floor.

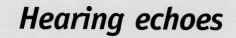

FISHY FACT

In 2008, a bottlenose dolphin rescued two sperm whales that were stranded on a beach, leading them back to the open sea.

DOLPHIN TALK

These friendly, playful animals can communicate with each other in an astonishing number of ways. Dolphins can "talk" with each other using different whistles and squawks. The way one dolphin touches another can show kindness or anger.

Playtime

Play is an important part of dolphin life. Playing together helps dolphins to build strong bonds with others in the group—and of course, to have fun. Dolphins are often seen playing with seaweed and leaping together in the splashing waves made by boats. A favorite activity is play-fighting with each other.

A long-finned pilot whale swims up to the camera with an open beak. It might be angry or just trying to play.

Whistling

In some species, each dolphin in a group has its own special whistle, which allows the others to recognize it. Chirping noises usually show excitement, while squawks are a sign of anger.

Touching

When two dolphins want to greet each other in a friendly way, they often rub their flippers together. If a dolphin needs help with a task, it may gently touch another group member on the side with its flipper. Among bottlenose dolphins, rubbing bodies together is a sign of affection. An older dolphin may calm down a younger one by rubbing it.

Spinner dolphins love to "bow ride," swimming in the waves made by a boat.

FISHY FACT

Dolphins usually stay close to sick or injured friends and family, even helping them swim to the surface to breathe.

KILLER WHALE

The killer whale is actually a very large dolphin. It is sometimes also called an orca. Despite its scary name, the killer whale does not attack people, although it is a skillful hunter of other sea creatures. It lives in all the world's oceans, remaining in cooler regions.

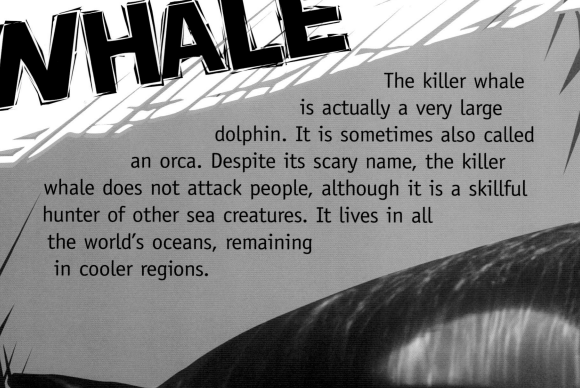

Hunting

These dolphins feed on a wide variety of prey, from fish and squid to large marine mammals and even other whales. Big groups of killer whales often work together when they are hunting. In the Southern Ocean, a pod of killer whales may use a clever plan to catch seals and penguins. Some of the whales jiggle the sea ice to disturb the seals and penguins resting on it. Other members of the pod catch the surprised animals as they leap into the water.

In Argentina, killer whales have learned how to grab sea lions from the beach then wriggle back into the water.

FISHY FACT

Sneaky killer whales in Alaska have learned how to steal fish caught on fishermen's lines, despite all the fishermen's attempts to stop them.

Family ties

Killer whales live in family groups of two to nine. It is common for an elderly mother to live with her children and grandchildren, together with their close relatives. Family pods often gather in bigger groups of up to 100.

The killer whale has a black upper body with a white underside and flanks.

A killer whale "spyhops" to have a look around.

INTO THE DEEP OCEAN

Warmth and light from the sun can reach only about 1,600 feet beneath the water surface. Below this, the water is cold and inky black. The deep, dark zones of the ocean form the largest region in the world—and we are still just learning about it. Some of the ocean's strangest animals lurk here.

Scientists explore the deep ocean using submersibles.

The dark zone

The region of the ocean that is untouched by sunlight is known as the dark zone. There are no plants and little food here. But some animals—such as fish, squid, jellyfish, and shellfish—manage to survive. Fish in the dark zone often have big jaws and sharp teeth as they cannot afford to let any prey escape. Some creatures have very large eyes to catch whatever small amount of light there is.

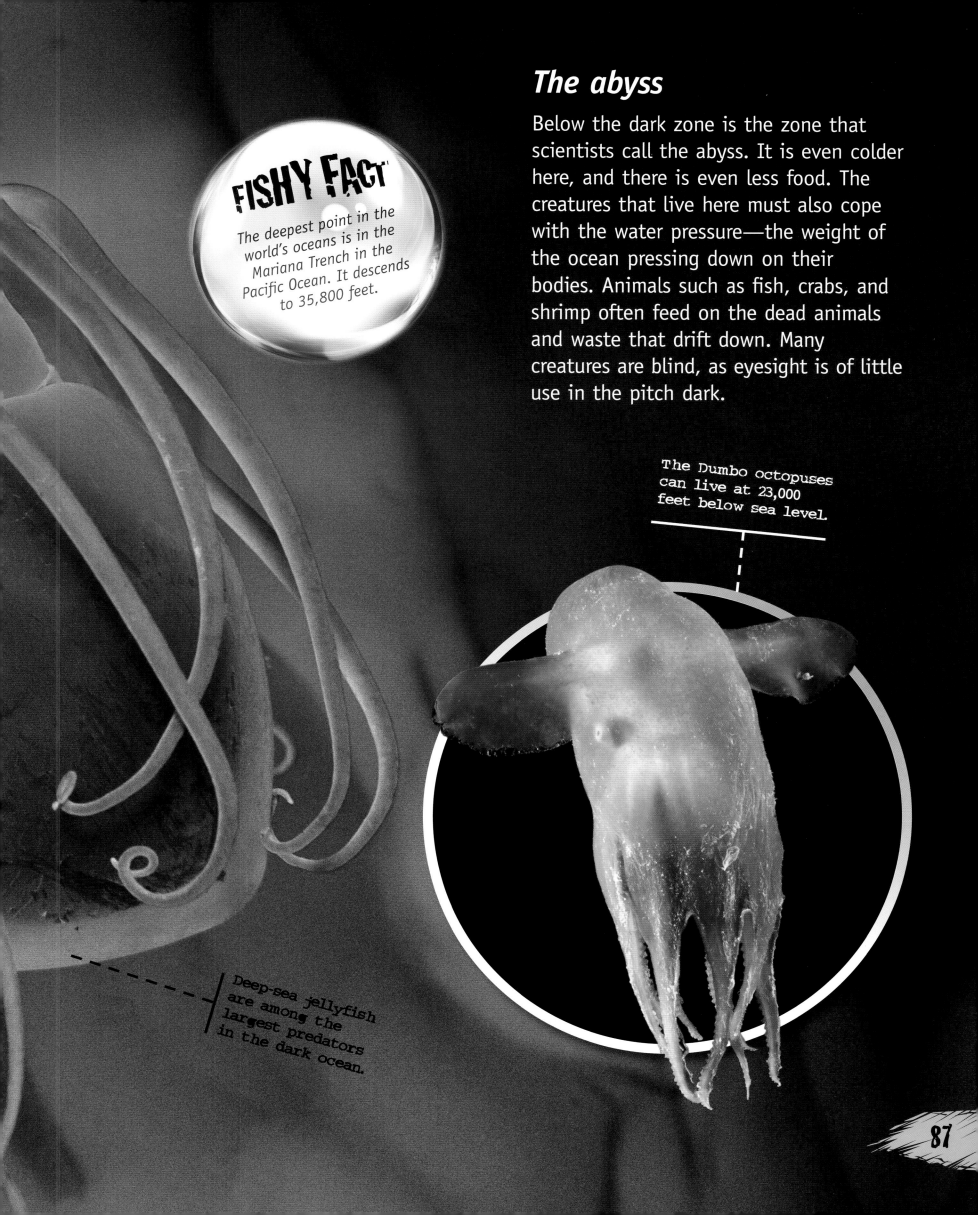

The abyss

Below the dark zone is the zone that scientists call the abyss. It is even colder here, and there is even less food. The creatures that live here must also cope with the water pressure—the weight of the ocean pressing down on their bodies. Animals such as fish, crabs, and shrimp often feed on the dead animals and waste that drift down. Many creatures are blind, as eyesight is of little use in the pitch dark.

FISHY FACT

The deepest point in the world's oceans is in the Mariana Trench in the Pacific Ocean. It descends to 35,800 feet.

The Dumbo octopuses can live at 23,000 feet below sea level.

Deep-sea jellyfish are among the largest predators in the dark ocean.

DEEPEST DIVERS

Not all creatures found in the deep ocean spend their whole lives there. Some are just visiting. Sperm whales, hatchetfish, and certain squid and jellyfish species are among the animals that move between the surface waters and the deep.

It takes a sperm whale 10 minutes to dive down every 3,300 feet.

Sperm whale

Like all whales, the sperm whale must spend much of its life near the surface so that it can breathe air into its lungs. But this whale is the deepest diver of all mammals, going down to 9,800 feet in its search for fish and squid. The sperm whale can hold its breath for up to two hours. This amazing diving skill may be due to a waxy substance called spermaceti inside the sperm whale's head. The spermaceti may help the whale change its ability to sink or float.

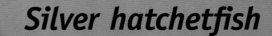

Silver hatchetfish

Like many ocean creatures, the hatchetfish spends its days in the deep but migrates at night to the food-filled surface waters. The hatchetfish's huge eyes help it to see in the dark ocean. On its belly there are rows of light-making organs. These lights help to camouflage the true shape of the hatchetfish and confuse its predators.

The Atlantic silver hatchetfish, also called the lovely hatchetfish, live in the warm and tropical areas of all oceans

The helmet jellyfish can live as deep as 23,000 feet, but moves to shallower waters to find food at night.

MAKING LIGHT

In the deep ocean, where the sun's light cannot reach, some creatures have developed an extraordinary ability. They make their own light using special organs on their body, called **photophores**. These lights can confuse predators, attract prey, or help find a mate.

With their glowing "fishing rod," sea devil anglerfish may live up to 10,000 feet below the surface.

Lanternfish

The lanternfish have photophores arranged in groups and rows on their bodies. Different species have different patterns, and so do males and females of the same species. Scientists think that the patterns help lanternfish spot a mate of the right species in the dark ocean. The photophores also help to camouflage the lanternfish. When seen from below, the lights make the lanternfish almost invisible when weak sunlight shines down from the surface.

90

Fishing for prey

Sloane's viperfish is one of many deep-sea fish that uses light to catch its prey. The first spine of its dorsal fin is very long and has a light-making organ on its end. This glowing fishing line attracts smaller fish. Deep-sea anglerfish also use shining lures, which grow out of their foreheads. These fish have huge, wide mouths and very stretchy stomachs. This allows them to swallow prey double their size.

The lanternfish can lash its tail from side to side to dazzle predators with its photophores.

Sloane's viperfish has such large teeth that they stick out when its mouth is closed.

DEEP-SEA PREDATORS

Deep-sea fish must compete with each other over a small amount of food. Many fish in the dark zone have huge jaws and even bigger stomachs, so that they can swallow prey much larger than themselves. Their fang-like teeth often point inward so that their prey has little chance of escape.

Tripod fish

The extraordinary tripod fish is one of the ocean's deepest-living fish. Three long, bony spines stick out from its tail and chest fins. The tripod fish stands on these "legs" on the seafloor. It faces into the current, waiting for shrimp and tiny fish to swim by.

It is too dark to see in the deep ocean, so the tripod fish uses its body to feel for its prey.

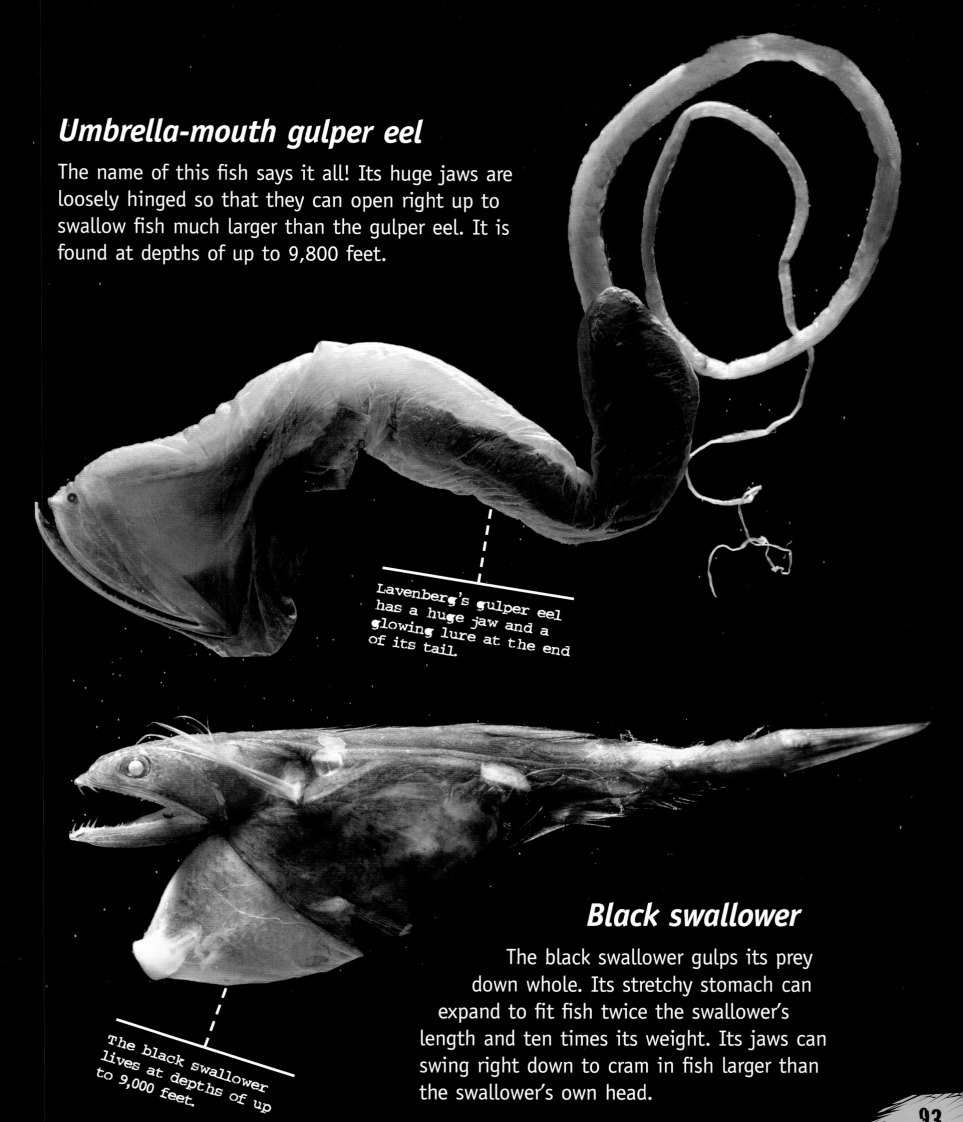

Umbrella-mouth gulper eel

The name of this fish says it all! Its huge jaws are loosely hinged so that they can open right up to swallow fish much larger than the gulper eel. It is found at depths of up to 9,800 feet.

Lavenberg's gulper eel has a huge jaw and a glowing lure at the end of its tail.

Black swallower

The black swallower gulps its prey down whole. Its stretchy stomach can expand to fit fish twice the swallower's length and ten times its weight. Its jaws can swing right down to cram in fish larger than the swallower's own head.

The black swallower lives at depths of up to 9,000 feet.

GIANT SQUID

Since they first traveled the seas, sailors have told tales about giant squid. They called them sea monsters, and it's no wonder. Giant squid can grow up to 43 feet long—that's the length of a bus. They can survive at depths of up to 3,300 feet.

The suckers on a giant squid's tentacles are lined with sharp teeth.

Many arms

Squid have eight arms and two long tentacles. The tentacles are armed with strong suckers that help the squid grasp its prey. A squid's mouth has a sharp beak that can kill and rip at fish and other squid. Adult giant squid are so huge and fierce that their only predators are sperm whales. The whales are sometimes left with round scars from the squid's suckers.

Like other squid and octopuses, the giant squid propels itself through the water by shooting jets of water out of its body.

This tough beak of a giant squid was found in a sperm whale's stomach.

Mysterious monster

Since the giant squid lives so deep in the ocean, we know very little about how it behaves. The first photographs of a live one were taken only in 2002. But we do know one amazing fact: the giant squid has the largest eyes of any living creature, reaching over 1 foot across. Such huge eyes are better at seeing in the murky depths.

There are probably eight species of giant squid, which live in all the world's oceans.

ANCIENT NAUTILUSES

The nautilus is a cephalopod, like octopuses, squid, and cuttlefish. Cephalopods have a large head and tentacles. The nautilus also has a shell, which it can pull right inside for safety. It has lived unchanged in the world's oceans for many millions of years.

Sense of smell

The nautilus has large eyes but it does not have good eyesight. It finds its prey using its keen sense of smell. The nautilus feeds on shrimp and fish, as well as dead animals that it finds on the seafloor. It grabs its prey using its tentacles, which have a very firm grip. Nautiluses sometimes have their tentacles ripped off rather than let go of something.

Nautiluses spend their days in the deep, but travel up to feed around coral reefs at night.

Spiral shell

A nautilus shell is a spiral shape. Inside, it is divided into chambers. A young nautilus has just four small chambers. As it grows and needs more room, a nautilus builds bigger and bigger chambers for itself, closing off the old chamber every time. An adult has 30 or more chambers.

A nautilus cannot swim any deeper than 2,600 feet below the surface. At this depth, its shell breaks because of the water pressure.

The chambered nautilus has up to 90 tentacles, which it uses to push prey into its mouth.

A spiraling nautilus shell is divided into chambers inside.

FISHY FACT
The beautiful shell of the chambered nautilus is becoming endangered. People catch it to sell the shell.

VENT LIFE

FISHY FACT

In the warm, mineral-rich water, vent clams grow 500 times faster than clams in other parts of the ocean.

In certain places there are cracks in the seabed, where water heated inside the earth spurts out. These are called hydrothermal vents. The hot water is full of **minerals** such as sulfur, which provides food for **bacteria**. Strange animals, which could survive nowhere else on the planet, feed on this bacteria and on each other.

Giant tubeworms

These huge worms have no mouth or stomach to eat with. Instead, they take food from bacteria that live inside them. Tubeworms protect their soft body by building a hard tube around themselves.

Far beneath the Ocean, sulfur pumping from a hydrothermal vent turns the water black.

Giant tubeworms can grow to 7 feet 10 inches tall.

Crabs scuttle around the vents, feeding on bacteria, tubeworms, clams, and mussels.

Zoarcid fish

These white fish, which can grow to 2 feet long, are one of the key predators around the vents. They feed on everything from tubeworms to vent crabs and shrimp.

COLD OCEANS

The North Pole lies in the Arctic Ocean. It is so cold here that much of the ocean is always covered by ice. The Southern Ocean surrounds the continent of Antarctica, at the center of which lies the South Pole. Animals that live in and around these oceans must survive in the coldest conditions on our planet.

The polar bear spends many months of the year at sea, living on the ice that covers the Arctic Ocean.

Southern Ocean

The Southern Ocean stretches from Antarctica to the southern edges of the Atlantic, Pacific, and Indian Oceans. In the ocean's coldest regions, closest to Antarctica, the water is covered by thick ice and the air temperature can sink to -22°F. But the Antarctic waters give life to a few thousand species of animals, including krill, fish, whales, seals and sea birds.

FISHY FACT

There are around 28,000 species of fish in the world, but only 200 of them live in Antarctic waters.

Arctic Ocean

The Arctic Ocean is the coldest of the world's oceans. The temperature of the surface water is just below freezing, at around 29°F. During the dark winter, little sunshine enters the water. But in the summer, the sun shines up to 24 hours a day. This sunlight gives life to plant plankton. These plants are a vital source of food for the animals that make their home here. These range from tiny animal plankton to the Arctic marine mammals: seals, whales, walruses, and polar bears.

The harp seal is one of the 12 species of marine mammals that regularly inhabit the Arctic.

KEEPING WARM

Antarctic fur seals rely on their thick coat to keep them warm.

Polar animals have to survive in the freezing water or battle with the icy, windy conditions on land. These animals have special adaptations, or features, to keep out the chill. These adaptations include extra-thick layers of fur, feathers, skin, and fat.

Blubber

Most marine mammals have a thick layer of fat, called blubber, under their skin. This insulates them from the cold, rather like putting on a sweater keeps us warm in the winter. The bowhead whale has the thickest blubber of any animal. It is 17–20 inches thick. The bowhead spends its entire life in and around Arctic waters.

Antifreeze

Many polar fish, such as Antarctic cod and icefish, are able to swim in icy waters because of a special antifreeze in their blood. This stops their blood from freezing so the fish can survive temperatures as low as 28°F.

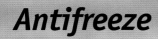

When ice covers the polar seas, it blocks the sunlight. Many polar fish have extra-large eyes to help them see in the darkened water.

The Antarctic icefish appears ghostly white because it has no red blood cells. This helps its blood flow freely in the cold.

Migration

Not all polar animals live in icy polar regions throughout the entire year. Many migrate to warmer regions during the bitterly cold winters. For example, snow geese spend their summer nesting in the Arctic, then fly down to the balmy southern USA in the winter.

The snowy sheathbill can puff out its extra-thick feathers to keep warm in the Antarctic winter.

103

COLD KRILL

There would be little life in the Antarctic without tiny floating plants, called plankton. These grow in the Southern Ocean in spring and summer. The plankton are food for millions of crustaceans called Antarctic krill. In turn, krill are the main food of over 20 species of fish and squid, 5 species of whales, 3 species of seals, and countless sea birds.

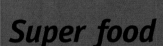

At 98 feet long, the blue whale is the world's largest animal. It feeds almost entirely on krill

Crustacean

Like other crustaceans, such as crabs and lobsters, the Antarctic krill has a hard external skeleton that protects its soft body. Krill grow to no more than 2.4 inches long, but live in large swarms of up to 1,000 animals in just 1 cubic foot of water. Krill catches plant plankton from the water using its special front legs. These legs act like tiny nets.

The Antarctic krill's large eyes help it to see in the dark water beneath the ice.

The Antarctic krill is a shrimp-like crustacean with an almost transparent body

Super food

Krill is a key species in the Antarctic. It is essential to the food chain, which starts with small plants and ends with giant whales. A blue whale gobbles up to 4 million krill every day. Crabeater seals eat hardly anything but Antarctic krill. All the crabeaters together eat 63 million tons of krill a year. That's the weight of 500,000 blue whales.

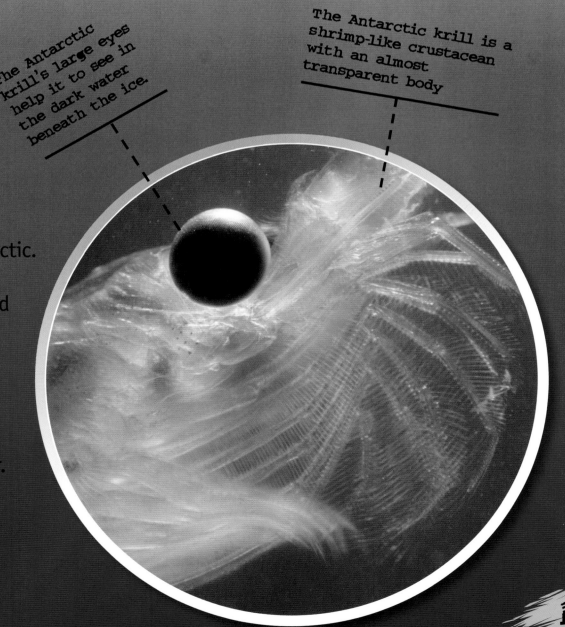

THE NARWHAL

The narwhal is known for the male's beautiful spiral tusk, which can grow up to 9.8 feet long. Centuries ago, merchants used to sell narwhal tusks for huge sums of money, claiming that they came from unicorns. The narwhal is a whale and it lives year-round in the Arctic.

The narwhal normally lives in a group of up to 10, but gathers in larger numbers when migrating.

The narwhal grows to 13–16 feet long, not including its tusk.

Spiral tusk

The male narwhal's tusk is actually a tooth. It grows straight out from the whale's upper jaw. The narwhal is one of very few animals to have a spiral tooth. It is certainly the only animal to have a straight tusk. All other tusks are curved. Usually only males grow a tusk. Very occasionally, a male grows two tusks, and sometimes a female narwhal grows a short one.

In spring, male narwhals can be seen clashing their tusks above the water. This is probably a sort of "tusking" competition.

What's it for?

Scientists have tried to work out exactly why the male narwhal needs a tusk. They have wondered if it is used to poke at the seafloor to find prey, for breaking the ice, or if it is used as a spear to kill prey. In fact, males probably just use their tusks to attract females and to impress other males.

ANTARCTIC SEALS

Six species of seal live in Antarctica: the Ross, Weddell, crabeater, elephant, leopard, and fur seals. With their thick layer of blubber, seals are well suited to polar life. They spend much of the year under the ice searching for food. At other times, they rest on beaches and ice floes, where they give birth to their young and catch a little sunshine.

Elephant seal

The largest seal in the world is the elephant seal. Males can weigh a whopping 8,800 pounds, which is as heavy as an Asian elephant. But in fact the species takes its name from the large nose of the male seals, which looks a bit like an elephant's trunk. When it is breeding time, one male elephant seal mates with a group of up to 50 females. He fights off any other males who try to come near.

A male elephant seal can make a loud coughing roar to scare away other males.

Weddell seal

This seal wins the prize for making longer and deeper dives than any other seal. It may go as deep as 2,000 feet hunting for squid, krill, and fish such as Antarctic cod. During the bitter, windy winters, Weddell seals prefer to stay underwater, where they breathe through holes in the ice.

Of all the world's mammals, Weddell seals live the furthest south, closest to the South Pole.

FISHY FACT

The large-eyed Ross seal is the smallest of the Antarctic seals, reaching no more than 8 feet long.

The leopard seal takes its name from the black spots on its throat.

WALRUS WARRIORS

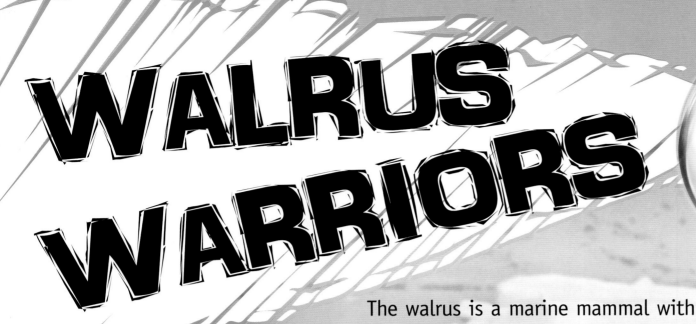

FISHY FACT

When a male walrus wants to attract a female, he sings to her by whistling, making bell sounds, and clacking his teeth.

The walrus is a marine mammal with large flippers. It is related to sea lions and seals, but walruses are easy to tell apart from their relatives because of their tusks, whiskers, and large size. The biggest males can weigh in at 4,400 pounds, which is as heavy as 25 men. Walruses live in and around Arctic waters.

A walrus's tusks are actually teeth that have grown up to 3 feet long.

Tusk tool

The walrus searches the seafloor for food such as crabs, tubeworms, and shrimp. Its tusks are the perfect tool for this task. The walrus drags its tusks through the sand and mud on the bottom, stirring it up. Then it digs up the food using its snout. A walrus also uses its tusks to break holes in the sea ice and for dragging itself out of the water.

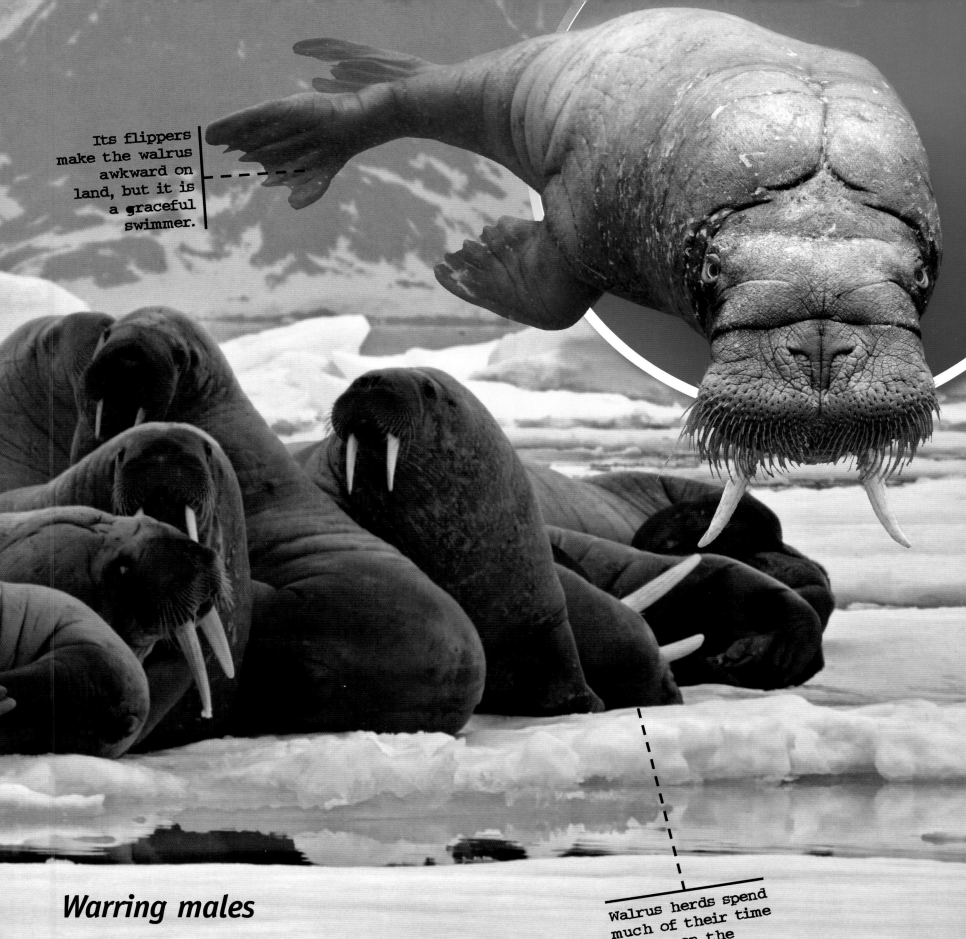

Its flippers make the walrus awkward on land, but it is a graceful swimmer.

Walrus herds spend much of their time resting on the Arctic ice.

Warring males

Both male and female walruses have tusks, but the male's tusks are usually thicker and longer. Male walruses can be very aggressive toward rivals in their herd. Sometimes they use their sharp tusks for fighting each other. At other times, they put on threatening displays, using their tusk size to scare off other males. The males with the biggest tusks are always leaders of their herd.

EMPEROR PENGUINS

The world's biggest penguin is the emperor, reaching an amazing 48 inches tall. That's as tall as an average seven-year-old. Emperors live in icy Antarctica, where large colonies huddle together to protect themselves from the cold.

Emperor parents

At the start of winter, adult emperor penguins walk up to 75 miles inland to nesting areas. Each female lays just one egg, which she transfers very carefully to her male partner. This transfer is difficult and sometimes the egg is broken. The exhausted female waddles to the sea to find food, while the male keeps the egg warm on his feet. After about 60 days, the egg hatches and the female returns to her partner and her chick.

In a crowded colony, parents and chicks use a wide range of calls to find each other and share food.

FISHY FACT
The smallest of the 17 penguin species is the fairy penguin, which is only 13 inches tall.

Ocean hunter

Like all penguins, the emperor cannot fly. It uses its strong wings like flippers as its dives and swims in the ocean, looking for fish and crustaceans to eat. The emperor's thick, waterproof feathers keep it warm in the sea and on the ice. Underneath its feathers is a layer of fat, known as blubber, which insulates it even more from the bitter Antarctic cold. The emperor is so well insulated with blubber that it is the fattest of all the penguin species.

Emperor penguins are expert swimmers, diving to depths of 1,300 feet in search of food.

PENGUIN COLONIES

All penguin species live south of the equator, but only four species live as far south as Antarctica. These species are the Adélie, chinstrap, emperor, and gentoo penguins. Penguins are sociable birds and live in large colonies. Penguin colonies are filled with the noise of birds calling to their chicks and their mates.

The chinstrap penguin is named for the black band under its chin, which makes it look like it is wearing a helmet.

FISHY FACT

Penguins walk awkwardly on land, so they often lie down on their bellies and toboggan over the ice instead.

Preening

In order to keep their feathers waterproof and windproof, penguins must preen them. They do this using a special oil that is made in a **gland** at the base of their tails. Using their bills, penguins spread the waterproof oil over their feathers. Sometimes a male and female breeding pair preen each other, or sometimes strangers in the colony do it for each other.

Group care

During the breeding season, penguins come ashore to nest in huge colonies. The largest colonies may have over a million birds. Living in a colony gives protection from predators and the Antarctic cold. When their chicks are a few weeks old, penguin parents must return to the sea to find food. Their chicks often huddle together for warmth. These groups of chicks are called *crèches*.

Penguins often hunt in groups, like these Adelie penguins.

Emperor penguin chicks cluster together in a creche.

THE COAST

The coast is where the land meets the sea. This is where waves crash on rocky shores or sandy beaches. From crabs scurrying across the sand to seabirds nesting on the cliffs, our shorelines are filled with life. Many coasts are surrounded by stretches of shallow water. It is in the shallows, rather than out in the deep sea, that most sea creatures live.

An octopus hides and many other creatures shelter in a rockpool on the shoreline.

In the shallows

The sunlit, shallow waters close to coasts are the perfect places for plants such as seaweed, mangroves, and seagrasses to grow. Seaweed called kelp can form great forests underwater. All these plants give food and shelter to animals from worms and crabs to turtles and dugongs.

Ghost crabs dig burrows in sandy beaches where they hide during both the cold winter and the midday summer heat.

Californian sealion swim through a kelp forest.

On the shore

Twice a day, the sea flows up the shore and then falls away again. These regular movements of the sea are called tides. Animals that live on the shoreline must cope with being at one moment exposed to the air and at the next plunged underwater again. To avoid being washed away, some invertebrates stick themselves to rocks or burrow into the sand. The shoreline is also the place where marine reptiles, seabirds, and many marine mammals go to breed or lay their eggs.

FISHY FACT

Hiding among rocks on the shoreline is a scuttling sea spider. Like the spiders that live on land, they often have eight legs.

LIVING IN A SHELL

When you find a shell washed up on the seashore, remember that it once contained an animal. It may well have been a soft-bodied animal called a mollusk. Around a quarter of all sea creatures are mollusks. Mollusks that live on the seashore include limpets, oysters, mussels, snails, and clams.

The inside of a pearl oyster's shell is made of iridescent mother-of-pearl

Pearl oysters

If you ever see a person wearing a pearl necklace, just think that the pearls came from a mollusk known as a pearl oyster. Pearls form when something irritating, such as a parasite, enters the mollusk's shell. The mollusk starts to cover the irritant with layers of nacre, which makes up the shell. Over time, this creates a pearl.

Hundreds of thousands of mussels have attached themselves to a beach in Norfolk, England. This is called a "mussel bed."

Limpets

Limpets creep over rocks on the seashore using their muscular foot. When they find little plants called algae, they scrape them up with their toothed tongue. To avoid getting washed away by breaking waves, limpets can clamp their shell down so hard on a rock that it is almost impossible to remove them. When we talk about someone being really stubborn we often say that they cling on like a "limpet."

Limpets have flat, cone-shaped shells.

FISHY FACT

The dog whelk is a species of sea snail. It bores holes in the shells of other mollusks then sucks them out.

SHY SEA HORSES

Despite their strange appearance, seahorses are actually fish. There are up to 47 species of seahorses, ranging in size from half an inch to 14 inches. They live in shallow, warmer waters close to the shore, staying near the shelter of coral reefs, seagrass, and mangroves.

A male spotted seahorse releases up to 1,500 baby seahorses into the water.

FISHY FACT
The world's slowest-moving fish is the dwarf seahorse, which has a very unimpressive top speed of 5 feet per hour.

Seahorse fathers

When a female seahorse lays her eggs, she puts them straight into a pouch on the male's body. Here they are kept warm and safe for up to a month. Throughout this time, the female returns every day to greet the male. The eggs hatch within his pouch, then the male pushes the newborns out into the sea. Now he has an empty pouch and the female can give him another batch of eggs.

A seahorse uses its tail to cling to seaweed.

Hide and seek

Seahorses take their name from their horse-like heads and necks. Unlike most fish, they swim upright rather than horizontally. In fact, they are pretty slow swimmers. To catch their prey, they hide among seagrass or coral, wrapping their tails around a frond to stay perfectly still. They even change their color to match their surroundings. Expertly camouflaged, they wait patiently for small crustaceans to swim by. Then they suck up their prey with their long snouts.

With its gray skin and red lumps, a pygmy seahorse is perfectly camouflaged among coral

AMAZING STARFISH

FISHY FACT

With its 50 arms, the Antarctic sun starfish wins the prize for the starfish with the most arms.

Starfish or sea stars are not actually fish: they are invertebrates. Starfish have at least five arms, growing from a disc-shaped body. They live on the seafloor of all the world's oceans, from the deep sea to beaches.

Polar starfish feed on mussels.

Terrifying stomach

A starfish's mouth is on the underside of its body. In many species, the starfish actually pushes its stomach outside its body to fetch prey. Sometimes, a starfish may even push its stomach into the shell of a clam or mussel. The stomach digests the food inside the shell, then is pulled back inside the starfish.

Astounding arms

The undersides of a starfish's arms are covered with tiny tube-like feet with suckers. The starfish can walk across the seafloor on these feet, reaching speeds of more than 3 feet per minute. The suckers are also used to grip prey, such as mussels, clams, oysters, and snails. If a predator pulls off one of a starfish's arms, the arm will usually grow back. Some species are able to regrow their whole body from a single arm.

A Common starfish's tubefeet move in waves, allowing the starfish to walk across the seafloor.

SPINY LOBSTERS

Spiny lobsters are crustaceans, which means they have a hard external skeleton, or shell. In order to grow, they must regularly shed their shell and make a bigger one. Like other lobsters, spiny lobsters have ten legs.

FISHY FACT

When they want to frighten a predator, spiny lobsters can rub the base of their antennae to make a loud rasping noise.

A line of spiny lobsters marches across the seafloor.

Follow your leader

At the first signs of winter, spiny lobsters move from the shallow water near shore into calmer, deeper water. The lobsters may walk hundreds of miles along the seafloor, moving in groups of up to 100,000. They walk in single file, with up to 60 lobsters in a line. Each lobster touches the one in front with its antennae so that it doesn't get lost. The lobsters find their way to their destination using the smell and taste of the changing substances in the water.

Scary antennae

Spiny lobsters get their name from the sharp spines that cover their bodies, making them too prickly for many predators. They can also wave their long, thick antennae to scare off attackers. They use smaller feelers called antennules to sense movement and substances in the water.

The shell of a painted spiny lobster is striped in white, pink, and black.

Spiny lobsters live in holes in rocks and coral reefs. At night, they creep out to find food such as crabs, clams, and snails.

125

CROCODILE ALERT!

The saltwater crocodile is the largest reptile in the world. At up to 23 feet long, these terrifying predators are really not something you want to bump into. They are found from northern Australia to the east coast of India.

FISHY FACT

The best way to avoid being attacked by a saltwater crocodile is to stay clear of its territory!

In northern Australia, watch out for the crocodile warning signs.

A saltwater crocodile spends much of its time basking in the sun. It can survive for months without food.

The saltwater crocodile's jaw muscles are so powerful that it has the strongest bite of any animal

Killer

These vicious crocs will attack any animal that strays into their territory. They wait until an animal comes close to the water, then race out to grab it. Adult salties have been known to eat everything from fish and frogs to kangaroos, monkeys, horses, sharks, and even people. Every year in Australia, one or two people are killed by saltwater crocs.

Know your enemy

The saltwater croc spends the tropical wet season in rivers and swamps inland. When these waters start to shrink in the dry season, it moves to the coast and sometimes swims far out to sea. Like other crocodiles, the "saltie" has a strong, streamlined body, which allows it to swim at up to 18 miles per hour. Its skin is covered in tough scales, rather like armor. Its teeth are deadly sharp for ripping its prey.

CALIFORNIA SEA LION

This clever sea lion is the fastest swimmer of all seals and sea lions. It can race at up to 25 miles per hour. You may have seen it performing in shows at the zoo or marine parks. But do you know the difference between a sea lion and a seal?

The California sea lion hunts for fish, squid, and clams.

Sea lion or seal?

Unlike true seals, sea lions have flaps over their ear holes. They also have longer and stronger flippers that they can use to walk on land. True seals have to wriggle along the ground, but sea lions can walk on all fours.

California sea lions are very sociable and may gather in colonies of several thousands.

Sea lion mothers

During breeding season, huge colonies of these sea lions gather along the west coast of the United States. Like other mammals, a sea lion mother feeds her pup with her own milk. When her pup is 10 days old, a mother has to start making trips to the sea to find food. While she is away, her pup will gather with other pups to play. Whenever a mother returns to land, she calls her pup with her own special call. A mother and pup can tell each other's calls from those of all the mothers and pups in the colony.

For the first year of its life, a pup totally depends on its mother for food.

THE DUGONG!

The dugong is a marine mammal, like whales and seals. But the strange fact is that the dugong is more closely related to an elephant than to the other sea mammals. Unlike most marine mammals, it only eats plants. The dugong always stays close to its favorite food: the seagrasses that grow along the coasts of the Indian and Pacific Oceans.

Gentle grazer

A dugong can grow to as long as 13 feet. It has paddle-like front flippers and a tail that looks rather like a dolphin's. Males have two tusks, which carry on growing throughout their lives. The dugong's large and strong upper lip helps it to feed on tough ocean grasses.

Dugongs graze on seagrasses, giving them the nickname "sea cows."

A female dugong gives birth only a few times in her life. She puts many years into caring for each calf.

A dugong can live for 70 years or more.

Caring for calves

A dugong mother gives birth in shallow water and pushes her calf to the surface to breathe straight away. A calf feeds on its mother's milk for at least 18 months. During this time it never moves from her side and may often ride on her back. A calf will only leave its mother when it is fully mature, at between six and nine years old.

FISHY FACT

In the Philippines, dugongs are believed to bring bad luck, while in Thailand, dugong tears are thought to make a love potion.

SUPER FLYERS

Most seabirds have very thick, waterproof feathers. They have webbed feet to help them chase their prey in the water. Some seabirds fly great distances over the oceans, hunting for food. These long-distance flyers have huge wings. They often spend much of the year at sea, coming to land only to lay their eggs and care for their chicks.

Giant petrels spend most of the year flying over the southern oceans but return to coasts and islands to nest.

Wandering albatross

This seabird has the largest wingspan of any bird, reaching up to 12 feet. It is able to glide through the air without flapping its wings for several hours at a time. When it catches sight of fish, squid, or crustaceans in the surface waters, it swoops to pluck them out with its beak. It is also well known for following boats, waiting for scraps to be thrown overboard.

The wandering albatross can cover 300 miles in just one day.

Great frigatebird

The great frigatebird has a wingspan of up to 7.5 feet. It spends most of its life at sea, snatching its prey from the water's surface while in flight. Its preferred diet is flyingfish, which leap right out of the water. This bird also has a nasty habit of chasing other seabirds and making them bring back up the food they have eaten so it can steal it.

A male great frigatebird puffs out his red throat to attract a female.

133

HIGH DIVERS

Some seabirds dive far beneath the waves to catch their prey. The best divers are often the worst flyers. In fact, the deepest divers are the penguins, which cannot fly at all. The emperor penguin wins hands down with dives of up to 1,770 feet beneath the water. Like penguins, some seabirds make their dives from the ocean's surface, while others plunge from dizzyingly high places in the air.

FISHY FACT

The puffin can hold up to 12 fish at once in its beak, arranging them with their heads pointing in alternate directions.

Gannets

Gannets are among the best plunge divers, crashing into the ocean at up to 60 miles an hour from heights of 100 feet. To cushion the blow as they hit the water, gannets have little air sacs under the skin of their face and chest.

Large colonies of thick-billed murres breed on cliffs, laying their eggs directly onto narrow ledges.

During the breeding season, an Atlantic puffin's beak turns orange, blue, and yellow.

Atlantic puffin

Although it moves clumsily on land, the Atlantic puffin is an excellent surface diver. It can descend to around 200 feet, pulling itself through the water with its powerful wings.

Thick-billed murre

Outside the penguin family, the thick-billed murre gets the award for deepest-diving bird. It usually dives from the water's surface, reaching depths of up to 689 feet.

Cape gannets dive-bomb a shoal of sardines.

OCEANS AT RISK

We need to start taking better care of our oceans. For too long, people have been dumping their waste in the water. Pollution belched into the air from factories is also threatening ocean life.

The ice covering the Arctic Ocean is shrinking. In fifty years, the Arctic may be totally clear of ice during the summer.

Global warming

When factories burn fuels such as coal, they release greenhouse gases into the air. Cutting down our forests also increases the amount of these gases in the air. The problem with greenhouse gases is that they trap heat in the atmosphere, making our planet warmer. This causes the ice at the poles to melt a little more every year. This damages the habitats of polar animals and sea creatures all around the world. As the oceans get warmer, coral reefs and mangroves, which are two of our most beautiful habitats, die.

Waste in the water

The waste that we put into the oceans is killing animals and destroying habitats. Garbage is thrown onto beaches and over the sides of ships. Pipes pour in sewage and dangerous chemicals from factories. Pollution dumped into rivers flows down into the sea. Ocean-going tankers carrying oil spill their load, killing thousands of animals at a time.

The warming of the oceans is causing some coral reefs to bleach, turning white and dying.

Oil from a spill covers a seabird's feathers and stops it from flying.

ENDANGERED SPECIES

More than 600 ocean species are officially at risk of becoming extinct, but the real number is probably much higher. Ocean habitats are being destroyed. Many species are being overfished and hunted.

Trade

Many species are endangered by trade. Some animals are captured alive for home fish tanks. Others are killed so that their shell, tusks, or skin can be sold as souvenirs, medicine, or goods such as jewelry. In order to protect them, it is illegal to trade in some animals, including giant clams, stony coral, sea turtles, and seahorses.

There are only 3,000 southern right whales left.

FISHY FACT

For centuries, whales were hunted for their meat and oil. Whaling is now banned, but eight species are still in danger of extinction.

The hawksbill turtle is hunted for its beautiful shell. It is sold as "tortoiseshell," even though it is illegal to do so.

The zebra shark is one of a hundred shark species that are threatened by overfishing.

Habitat loss

When habitats like reefs are damaged, it puts at risk all the animals that depend on them. The green turtle is just one of those animals. On top of the threats to the reefs where it swims, the beaches where it lays its eggs are affected by building.

Overfishing and hunting

Overfishing is when we catch too many of one species of fish for food. The species never gets time to breed and build up its numbers again. To stop overfishing, fishermen are given limits on how many fish they can catch of a certain species.

GLOSSARY

Algae
simple, plant-like living things, such as seaweeds

Antennae
feelers that may be used for touching, tasting, or sensing movement

Antivenom
medicine used to treat venomous bites and stings

Bacteria
tiny, simple organisms that live in, on, and around most living and non-living things

Camouflage
patterns, colors, or body shapes that allow animals to blend into their surroundings

Colony
a group of animals living together

Crustacean
an animal with a hard external skeleton, such as a crab or lobster

Dorsal fin
fin on the back of a fish, whale, or dolphin

Endangered
in great danger of becoming extinct

Extinct
when the last remaining animal of the species has died

Fossil
trace of a plant or animal that lived long ago, preserved in the Earth's crust, as in rock or ice

Gills
the special parts of a fish's body that absorb oxygen from the water

Gland
organ in the body that makes a special substance, either for the animal to use or to get rid of

Global warming
a rise in the average temperature of Earth's atmosphere

Habitats
areas where an animal or plant normally lives

Invertebrate
an animal without a backbone

Mammal
an animal with a backbone, lungs to breathe air, and some body hair; female mammals make milk to feed their young

Marine
living in the sea

Minerals
natural, solid substances, such as gold or sulfur

Mollusk
a soft-bodied animal with a muscular foot or tentacles, often with a hard outer shell

Paralyze
to make an animal unable to move

Parasite
an organism that grows and feeds on or in another living thing

Pectoral fins
pair of fins on either side of a fish, whale, or dolphin

Photophores
organs on an animal's body that make light

Plankton
plants, animals, and other living things that are not able to swim against the water current

Pollution
harmful substances that are released into the environment

Predator
an animal that feeds on other animals

Prey
an animal that is hunted or captured for food

Reptile
an animal with lungs to breathe air and an outer covering of scales or plates

School
group of fish or other marine animals all swimming in the same direction

Shoal
group of fish that have come together to feed or nest

Species
group of animals or plants that look and behave very similar to each other; members of the same species can breed together

Streamlined
with a smooth shape that moves easily through water

Tentacles
long limbs that are used for feeling, grabbing, and feeding

Tropical
in a region around the Earth's equator, where the weather is warm all year round

Venom
poison made by an animal that is given to its victim by biting

INDEX

INDEX